THE COMPLETE BOOK OF THE
RUGBY WORLD CUP
1999

THE COMPLETE BOOK OF THE
RUGBY WORLD CUP
1999

EDITED BY
IAN ROBERTSON

Photographs by
Colorsport

Hodder & Stoughton
in association with
Scottish Life

First published in Great Britain in 1999 by
Hodder and Stoughton
A division of Hodder Headline

10 9 8 7 6 5 4 3 2 1

A CIP catalogue record for this book is available from the British Library

ISBN 0 340 75126 6

Produced by Lennard Books
A division of Lennard Associates Limited
Mackerye End, Harpenden, Herts AL5 5DR

Editor (for Lennard Books): Chris Marshall
Production editor: Ian Osborn
Design: Design 2 Print
Cover design: Paul Cooper Design
Reproduction: Radstock Repro

The photographs in this book were taken by the team of Colorsport photographers who
followed the 1999 RWC finals: Colin Elsey, Stuart MacFarlane, Andrew Cowie,
Matthew Impey, Paul Roberts, Simon Baker and Steve Bardens.

A special thanks to Mark Leech for the photograph of
Stephen Larkham's dropped goal on page 127.

Printed and bound in Great Britain by
Butler & Tanner Ltd, Frome and London

Hodder and Stoughton
A Division of Hodder Headline
338 Euston Road, London NW1 3BH

Grateful thanks to all the writers who contributed to this book.
They were all heavily involved in covering Rugby World Cup 1999 in their normal roles
as journalists or broadcasters but still compiled specially commissioned work for this project
and managed to meet every deadline.

Also full marks to our photographers at Colorsport for their tremendous efforts in producing
their usual vast collection of excellent pictures. And finally, a word of gratitude to the
willing band of angels who burned the midnight oil on a many occasions to deliver the manuscript
week by week throughout the tournament. They were enthusiastically led by Jeni Sargeant
who was willingly supported by Clare Robertson and Cathy Mellor.

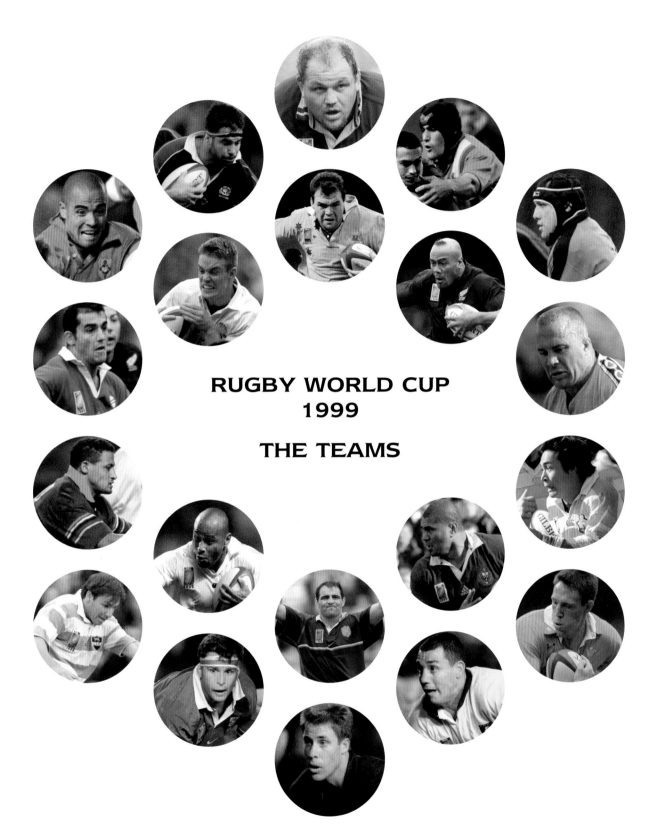

RUGBY WORLD CUP
1999

THE TEAMS

AHEAD
OF

As an independent UK law firm, McGrigor Donald works with businesses of all shapes and sizes, adding value through focused advice and the highest standards of client service Whatever your business goals, we can help you achieve them.
Quality, commitment and the will to win are at the heart of everything we do.

THE PACK

McGRIGOR DONALD SOLICITORS

SHARING THE VISION

Contents

great performers

Scottish Life
the **PENSION** company

Good training, excellent teamwork, outstanding results – they've all combined to win us five-star service awards for five years running. A great performance from our own 'Dream Team'

S cottish Life has been involved with rugby for many years, at international, club and youth levels. I am therefore delighted that Scottish Life has supported the production of this book which celebrates the last major sporting event of the Millennium.

The fourth Rugby World Cup has produced some tremendous examples of the sport at its best. Both technical ability and levels of fitness have reached new heights – indeed, if rugby excellence could be measured as precisely as in athletics, this year's rugby Olympics would surely have produced an impressive list of new world records.

This book is a fine record of the action, colour and passion enjoyed at the 1999 Rugby World Cup. I am sure rugby fans worldwide will greatly enjoy reading it now, but also value the book in future years as a lasting record of a great tournament.

Brian Duffin
Group Chief Executive
Scottish Life

foreword

Eat

Sleep

Drink

Bank

HSBC. It's a sure sign that you're dealing with a world-class financial services organisation.

We've been around for more than 130 years. Now we're in 79 countries and territories, serving over 20 million customers.

Those are the numbers. But it's our integrity and common sense solutions that you can truly count on.

Wherever you are in the world, wherever you are in your life, HSBC will be there for you.

HSBC

YOUR WORLD OF FINANCIAL SERVICES

Issued by HSBC Holdings plc

Introduction

The Biggest Rugby Show on Earth

Alastair Hignell

The Millennium Stadium during the Opening Ceremony of RWC 1999, which featured 1500 performers, including Shirley Bassey, Catatonia and Ladysmith Black Mambazo.

Coaches plan their campaigns around it. Players plan their careers around it. It's hard to believe that Rugby World Cup has been with us only 12 years. If the first tournament, held in Australia and New Zealand in 1987, was a slightly self-conscious step in the dark, Rugby World Cup 1999 was to be a gloriously self-confident celebration of the sport.

That first World Cup had featured 16 invited teams. The same number had to qualify for the second and third tournaments. By 1999 the game's authorities felt confident enough of the sport's spread and appeal to increase to 20 the number of teams competing in the final stages of the tournament. Whereas the top eight nations in previous World Cups had been guaranteed places at the next event, it was decided this time that only 1995 winners South Africa, runners-up New Zealand, third-placed France and 1999 host country Wales would qualify

as of right. The rest, including 1991 champions and runners-up Australia and England, would have to earn their places in the 1999 event.

Sixty-five teams took part in 133 matches until, by an incredibly complex process, 16 teams had won the right to join the pre-selected four. There were next to no surprises. Of the teams that had previously played in the finals, only Zimbabwe and the Ivory Coast failed to make it. Tonga, one of the 1987 originals, made it back through a 'repechage' system that required them to play off against

Following pages: The Millennium Stadium at dusk. Constructed on the site of the legendary Cardiff Arms Park, it provided a magnificent arena for Rugby World Cup 1999.

Tonga had to qualify for the finals through the repechage system, having finished bottom of the tough South Pacific Zone, whose other members were Australia, Samoa and Fiji.

Morocco, Georgia, the Netherlands and Korea. The United States and Fiji, who had both missed out in 1995, made welcome returns, while Spain and Uruguay were first-time visitors to the final stages.

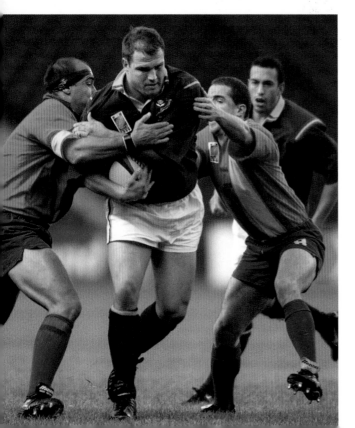

The decision to have 20 teams in Rugby World Cup 1999 made the logic of siting a pool in each of the Five Nations inescapable. The problem of reducing to eight teams for the quarter-finals was solved by the introduction of an extra round, the quarter-final play-offs, for the pool runners-up and the best third-placed side. In practice, that meant an increase in the number of matches from 32 to 41 compared with 1995, and an increase in the duration of the tournament from 31 days to 37.

Wales had the honour of staging the first and last matches, and to celebrate they tore down the National Stadium in Cardiff and built another one in its place. The £125 million Millennium Stadium, with its retractable roof and its removable playing surface, was trumpeted as the greatest rugby stadium in the world, but it very nearly didn't get built on time. Throughout the summer, stories abounded of strikes, delays and contingency plans, but every deadline was met in the nick of time. There was no roof, and room only for 27,000, when world champions South Africa came to call at the end of June, but when the concrete dust had cleared on an inspired home victory, and the hard hats raised to the perseverance of the building as well as the playing team, it did at last seem as

World Cup finals newcomers Spain (in red), who will play in the 1999-2000 European Shield for club sides, were drawn against world champions South Africa in Pool A of RWC 1999.

if the vision would become a reality. August internationals against Canada and France confirmed that the believers had triumphed over the doom-mongers. Everything was going to be all right on judgment day.

It wasn't just the city of Cardiff and the economy of Wales that were set to get a boost from the first World Cup of the professional era. The building of the Millennium Stadium was due to provide 4500 man-years of employment, while hotels and tour operators were set to make millions. So too was Rugby World Cup. The 1987 tournament, hastily organised and initially resented in some rugby quarters, had realised a profit of a comparatively measly $5.3 million. By 1991, when the northern hemisphere provided favourable time zones for advertisers who themselves had woken up to the pulling power of an event that was already trumpeting itself as the third largest on the planet, that figure had multiplied sevenfold to $37.7 million. By 1995 and the first, and so far only, World Cup to have been held in a single country and under a single legal system, the profit had swelled to $46 million. On Rugby World Cup's return to the northern hemisphere, the game's authorities were confident of breaking the $100 million mark.

The projections for television audience figures were equally encouraging. The 1987 tournament had been broadcast to just 17 countries to a cumulative audience of 300 million viewers. One hundred and three countries took television pictures of the 1991 competition; 1.75 billion people tuned in. By 1995, the Rugby World Cup was broadcast to 124 countries to put the event ninth in an all-time TV popularity league – sixth as a single sports event – with a cumulative audience of 2.65 billion viewers. For 1999, the marketing men were talking of three billion viewers from 140 countries.

Actual interest, as opposed to television viewing figures, was also predicted to soar. Only 600,000 spectators had attended Rugby World Cup 1987, with under half of that number turning up for pool games. Better marketing, and the extra tourist attractions provided in Europe, had swelled that latter figure to 650,000 in 1991, with a milllion spectators attending the matches in person. That last figure, surprisingly in view of the perceived greater capacity of South Africa's Test-playing grounds, didn't increase significantly in 1995, while the actual attendance at pool games was slightly down. Yet, admittedly for a greater number of matches, Rugby World Cup 1999 was confidently expecting a million fans through the turnstiles at pool games, with an extra five million witnessing the knockout matches.

In addition the authorities were making plans for an explosion in interest from other sections of the media. Where 400 journalists and photographers had reported on the first World Cup, one and a half times as many had described the 1991 tournament. Nine hundred took in South Africa in 1995; over 1400 were expected in 1999.

The first Rugby World Cup of the professional era, the last major sports event of the Millennium, showed every indication of setting new marks, of breaking new records. But could it push back the boundaries on the field as well? That, thankfully, was up to the players…

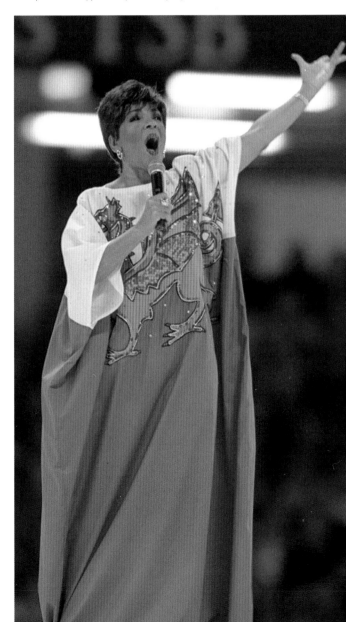

Welsh diva Shirley Bassey in full voice at the Opening Ceremony on 1 October, at which she performed 'The World in Union' with operatic baritone Bryn Terfel.

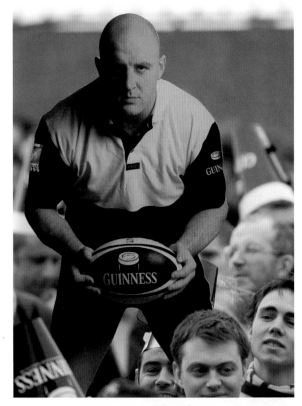

International Cap

A refreshing world class player

 **FOSTER'S**®

Pool A

A Pool of Two Halves

Bill McLaren

South Africa's scrum half Werner Swanepoel tries to thread his way between fly half Aitor Etxeberria and lock forward Jose Miguel Villau of Spain.

The main talking point in Pool A – from which South Africa's and Scotland's qualification was regarded by most people as a foregone conclusion – was about the disappointing attendances at the games in Scotland that brought forth strong criticism of the Rugby World Cup's organisation over the cost of tickets, not to mention the somewhat inconvenient kick-off times. Even the Scotland v South Africa game, which was a thoroughly entertaining affair, did not play before a capacity audience but one 10,000 short at 57,612. Elsewhere the matches took place in the absence of big-crowd atmosphere. Murrayfield's huge 67,500-capacity stadium had only 9463 for Scotland v Uruguay, 4769 for South Africa v Spain and 17,593 for Scotland v Spain.

One would have thought also that their previous experience of allocating rugby games to football grounds would have convinced the organisers that rugby folk do not take kindly to such an arrangement. Thus only 3500 people turned up to see South Africa take on Uruguay at the national football ground, Hampden Park, Glasgow, a situation that seemed to affect the world champions, who registered only five tries in a 39-3 victory. In sharp contrast, when the opening Pool A game brought together the group's 'minnows', Uruguay and Spain, at the Gala Club's ground, Netherdale, in the Scottish Border country, the audience numbered only 3761, but in the smaller stadium it provided a very enthusiastic and noisy gathering, giving some weight to the opinion that more club rugby grounds should have been used for those pool games rather than the spacious and untenanted Murrayfield and Hampden Park.

Above: Jacobus Petrus 'Os' du Randt at work against Scotland. Scrummaging against this 6ft 3in, 20-stone prop 'is like trying to shift the Empire State Building'.

In any event that opening game not only provided some exciting passages between countries whose rugby situation is still essentially amateur but also some delightful harmonised singing by the Uruguayan support whenever their side scored. The banter was friendly and, as the Spanish manager, Alfonso Mandado, said: 'The important thing is to be here in the finals; the results are secondary.' Certainly Netherdale always will have a warm place in Uruguayan hearts, for their reaction to beating Spain by 27-15 was to convey the impression that they had indeed won the World Cup!

Spain depended largely on their Ukrainian-born stand-off Andrei Kovalenco, who scored all their points with five penalty goals, whereas Uruguay fancied themselves as scrummagers and seemed happy to scrummage all day, not least when one such scrummage produced their opening try in fairy-tale circumstances.

Diego Ormaechea, veterinary surgeon, captain of Uruguay, and oldest player ever to take part in an RWC finals – not to mention scorer of Uruguay's first World Cup finals try.

The oldest player ever to take part in the World Cup finals, Diego Ormaechea, was the Uruguayan captain. He was a 40-year-old veterinary surgeon with three children who had played international rugby for 20 years and was gaining his sixty-third cap. He was the Uruguayan No. 8. Imagine his delight and that of his colleagues when he registered Uruguay's first ever try in a World Cup finals game with a cleverly timed scrummage pick up and scoring dive for his fourteenth international try. It gave the veteran more pleasure than the award of an old-age pension would have done.

For a player of such vintage, Ormaechea had an enviable work rate and clearly was a popular father figure to the Uruguayan side, whose winning margin owed much also to two spectacular clinching tries by full back Alfonso Cardossa and right wing Jean Menchaca, who scorched over 70 metres for a sensational finale. Nor could the Uruguayan coach, Daniel Herrera, resist a crack at Uruguay's big South American rivals Argentina: 'They won only one game in three Rugby World Cups. For us to win our first game in our first World Cup participation is just like a miracle.' It was indeed a splendid achievement by the Uruguayans, who have to select their national side from playing personnel numbering only 1200.

Turning our attention now to the Springboks. Jacobus Petrus du Randt is an extremely large citizen out of Elliot in South Africa who is nicknamed 'Os', Afrikaans for Ox, which is what Os resembles, at least in size. He is the kind of fellow who when he stands up blocks out the sunlight. Not surprisingly, Os revels in scrummaging, for it is in the darkened recesses of that particular phase of the Rugby Union game that he can use his size, 6ft 3ins and 20 stones, as well as his technical expertise to provide his country's scrummage with a handsome advantage. Scrummaging for any length of time in direct opposition to Os is like trying to shift the Empire State Building – and just as tiring. So when Scotland opted for their opening World Cup game, against South Africa, to place in direct opposition to Os a narrow, stocky little soul called George Graham who used to play for Stirling County in the shadow of that hilltop monument to Scotland's great warrior William Wallace, there was some concern that Scotland's scrummage would need oil on its hinges as the mighty Os got to work on GG, who

Springbok wing Pieter Rossouw tries to shake off Scottish lock Scott Murray. Like so many southern hemisphere backs, Rossouw is big, strong and a powerful runner.

once played as a stand-off for Carlisle Rugby League Club. They need not have worried. Graham bears a distinct resemblance not only in his stocky build but in his 'up and at 'em' attitude to a famous Scottish and Lions prop forward predecessor, Ian McLauchlan, who caused raised eyebrows and no little discomfort by, on several occasions, hanging up to dry with their feet off the ground far heavier and bigger opposing prop forwards. In those days you could do that without penalty. Not now.

GG didn't exactly hang Os up to dry, but he held his own by forcing the big amiable South African to scrummage at awkward low levels. In any event the Scottish scrummage stood its ground. Even when South

Scotland's Budge Pountney runs into South Africa's Percy Montgomery, as Kenny Logan arrives in support. Logan, the Scots' goal-kicker, booted 16 points in the game.

Africa went for a series of pushover scrummages the Scots denied them, and Os actually was replaced before George. What was even more pleasing to Scottish eyes was that pressure in the scrummage did not prevent Graham from lighting up the action with occasional typical robust charges into enemy lines with a touch of 'yoiks' and 'tally-ho' to his actions.

At the same time 'Big Os' took credit for just slogging away against an awkward opponent, but in a manner that bore out Os' philosophy: 'It's not whether you win or lose, it's how you play the game.' Although South Africa won 46-29 and by six tries to two, the Scots yet hinted at an ability to make a big impact, provided they could eliminate the punting and first-up tackle errors that hindered their effort. Gregor Townsend had one of those days with his punting when targets were not hit, as, for instance, when one clearance was run back by Percy

South Africa's midfield duo of Brendan Venter (12) and Robbie Fleck both got onto the scoresheet against Scotland, in the 23rd and 43rd minutes respectively.

Montgomery, Brendan Venter and Deon Kayser for a super try by Robbie Fleck. On another occasion Townsend's punt ignited Montgomery and Pieter Rossouw, and ruck ball then sent the massive Ollie le Roux thundering over, Ollie having replaced Os after 48 minutes. Ollie's final scoring dive measured high on the Richter Scale and indeed rattled the nearby rooftops. The final insult and crushing blow followed soon after when Townsend's lob pass was not gathered in by Scott Murray, a former Scottish Schools basketball international, and Kayser scooped and sprinted 40 yards for the fourth of South Africa's six tries.

It further hindered Scotland's cause that with South Africa leading 18-16 they lost John Leslie with ankle damage, thus being deprived of their most creative back, who has a gift for helping colleagues to play, through his option choice and his ability to offload ball profitably out of tackle situations. The 35-year-old Alan Tait boosted his try tally to 17 in 25 cap internationals by, once again,

showing brilliance in selection of running angles in latching on to Townsend-crafted feed in cluttered confines. Townsend had a disappointing day with his punt placements, but in making Tait's try he showed once again his instinctive feel for opening up the tightest defence.

Yet the try of the day, and perhaps of the entire World Cup, as far as simplicity and effectiveness were concerned was of Springbok creation. From scrummage ball Joost van der Westhuizen made a feint lateral burst to the right whilst leaving the ball for Bobby Skinstad to pick up and feed Brendan Venter powering up the left. Even the gutsy Gary Armstrong just couldn't prevent the try.

The Scots, who matched their rivals in the forward exchanges, were unfortunate in conceding a try to André Venter, although the incident underlined that old advice to keep playing until the referee blows his whistle.

Former Scottish Schools basketball international Scott Murray gathers in against finals newcomers Uruguay, who were playing their first game ever at Murrayfield.

Montgomery was fractionally late in his tackle on Scotland's wing Cameron Murray. Some Scots hesitated, but the referee, Colin Hawke of New Zealand, didn't blow, and Fleck sent Venter home.

The exciting Five Nations champions versus reigning World Cup holders contest lit up the World Cup after the somewhat disappointing opening shots fired by Wales and Argentina, in which the Pumas played percentage rugby and Wales just didn't get that midfield gear to mesh. Scotland and South Africa therefore set the tone in entertainment value for the rest of the World Cup. The lead changed hands five times, and South Africa were still in arrears going into the last quarter, in which they scored four tries for victory by 46-29. They sent out a clear message that they were in good nick for defending the William Webb Ellis Trophy they won at home in 1995, even in the injury absence of their key midfield player Henry Honiball, for whom Jannie de Beer deputised so well with a potent mix of fast punt and throw.

Scotland's rugby director, Jim Telfer, felt that on John Leslie's departure the Scots had sought to force their game a bit too much when 'we still could have played percentage rugby'. The quality of Scotland's performance was summed up by South Africa's replacement prop Ollie le Roux: 'They have come on by leaps and bounds. It was really a tough match for us, much harder than the last time we played them.'

Having lost their opening game, Scotland then had to ensure that they won the next two in order to be sure of qualifying for the later stages of the competition. This they did with comfortable victories against Uruguay (43-12) and Spain (48-0), but they were subjected to some criticism, especially after the Uruguay match, in which they yet scored six tries to none.

The South Americans are entirely an amateur side except for their 18-stone Bristol prop, Pablo Lemoine, but they tackled like the crack of doom, they frequently denied Scotland the quick later-phase ball with which they might have stitched together some attractive passages of continuous handling action, and they were prepared with a big pack to scrummage until the cows came home. All that plus some Scottish handling errors ensured that this would be no 80-points affair as some had predicted and

Gordon Simpson celebrates scoring the third of Scotland's six tries against Uruguay. The South Americans did not roll over – indeed they 'tackled like the crack of doom'.

that the Uruguayans would emerge from their first visit to Murrayfield in their first venture to the World Cup finals with considerable credit.

Perhaps the size of the audience proved uninspiring to the Scottish side, but it took them ages to achieve some flow, partly because of handling vulnerability alongside some ferocious Uruguayan tackling. It is no easy task to achieve continuity against a side that aims essentially at damage limitation and therefore at preventing their opponents from actually playing. The Uruguayans embraced this percentage strategy with vigour and focus.

It was hardly surprising that Scotland's two opening tries resulted from Gregor Townsend being more on song with his punting than he had been against South Africa. His penalty to touch enabled Stuart Grimes to rise like a rocketing pheasant to provide line-out ball with which Martin Leslie was driven over. Then Gordon Simpson won line-out ball and Leslie's touch-line thrust opened the way for Gary Armstrong to score. Strong Scottish scrummaging and drive and fast rucked ball put Simpson

Below: Wide open spaces in the stands at Murrayfield as South Africa take on Spain. Low attendances were a feature of Pool A for a variety of reasons.

over, and when Kenny Logan shot up the left touch line, Glenn Metcalfe was on hand to touch down. The last two tries in Scotland's 43-12 win were by Townsend and hooker Rob Russell, who had replaced Gordon Bulloch after ten minutes. The Uruguayan points stemmed from the boot of the stand-off and orchestrator, Diego Aguirre, with three penalty goals, and that of their lively little scrum half, Federico Sciarra, with one.

Although the Springboks registered seven tries in a 47-3 win over Spain it was far from a dazzling display by the reigning world champions, partly, no doubt, because of the lack of atmosphere and crowd reaction from an audience of under 5000 and a huge gap in the stands. It took the Springboks 29 minutes to open their account, which was as much due to their own failure to stitch the bits and pieces together as to the tenacious defence of the Spanish side. Although the South Africans spent almost

Springbok centre Brendan Venter pulls away from Uruguay's Sebastian Aguirre. Venter was later sent off for alleged dangerous footwork and was banned for 21 days.

the entire second half in Spanish territory they still managed to score only four tries in that time. It was their captain of the day, André Vos, who eventually opened the South African try account after some typical sand-dancing by their full back, Breyton Paulse. That illusive little fellow made the second try too by streaking out of defence to send scrum half Werner Swanepoel home. Swanepoel, who has the unenviable task of understudying such a star as Joost van der Westhuizen, then created the opening for a try by Anton Leonard for a 21-0 half-time lead. Further South African tries came from Vos (his second), Pieter Muller and Bobby Skinstad, and six were converted by Jannie de Beer. During the second half the Springboks demonstrated the power of their scrummaging for a penalty try, and the only Spanish score was a penalty by substitute stand-off Ferran Velasco. Yet the Spaniards were given such an ovation at the end by the vociferous support that they came out from the dressing room to take a second bow. At 47-3 they reckoned they had done pretty well in tries limitation – and indeed they had.

Five days after that win over Spain the Springboks took on Uruguay in unfamiliar conditions before a sparse crowd at Hampden Park that clearly inhibited both sides but especially the South Africans, accustomed as they have been to playing before animated and responsive audiences. Certainly the Springboks looked anything but world champions as they were hustled and bustled out of their rhythm and team play into a series of errors. Not only that but Brendan Venter, their experienced midfield strongman, was sent off by Australian referee Peter Marshall for alleged dangerous footwork that seemed to have been witnessed by the Australian touch judge Steve Walsh. Venter's dismissal was of special concern, because in the later stages of the tournament, if two sides play a drawn game, the issue could be decided after extra time on the number of players sent off during the tournament. In what was described in one newspaper account as 'a shabby display', the Springboks emerged victors by 39-3 through tries by Robbie Fleck, van der Westhuizen, Kayser and van den Berg (two) and four conversions and two penalty goals by de Beer to a penalty goal by Aguirre.

When Scotland took on Spain in the last of the Pool A games, they knew that the South Africans would top the pool and, therefore, that Scotland probably would face Samoa in the quarter-final play-offs and then almost certainly the All Blacks in the quarter-finals, whilst the Springboks would meet England at Twickenham.

Bryan Redpath, standing in for Gary Armstrong as scrum half and captain against Spain, runs at Jose Miguel Villau (4) and Jose Ignacio Zapatero during Scotland's 48-0 win.

Scotland's coaching hierarchy decided to ring the changes for the Spanish match so that the 21-year-old Chris Paterson, nephew of Duncan Paterson, former Scottish scrum half and selection chairman, was awarded his first cap at full back. Jamie Mayer and James McLaren were paired in midfield, Duncan Hodge took over at stand-off, 6ft 6ins blonde New Zealander Cameron Mather gained a second cap as flanker, and to mark his fiftieth cap as a prop, Paul Burnell, who first played against England in 1989, led out the Scottish team. Burnell became the tenth Scottish player to reach the 50-caps milestone, the others being Sandy Carmichael, Andy Irvine, Jim Renwick, Colin Deans, Gavin Hastings, Scott Hastings, Craig Chalmers, Tony Stanger and Doddie Weir. In gaining caps also against Samoa in the quarter-final play-off and against New Zealand in the quarter-final, Burnell, with 52 caps, thus passed Sandy Carmichael's mark as the most-capped Scottish prop of all time. Scotland's captain, Gary Armstrong, also joined the 50-caps brigade when he took the field against Samoa.

Powerful scrummaging gave Scotland a distinct edge against the Spaniards. One squeeze brought a penalty try for taking down the scrummage, another launched Mather for the first of his two tries. Scotland were 22-0 up at the break following a try by another Kiwi, Shaun Longstaff, and their other tries in a 48-0 victory were from McLaren, Cameron Murray and Duncan Hodge, who also potted five conversions and a penalty goal for 18 points. Perhaps the most entertaining aspect of the scoring was the try scored by winger Cameron Murray after the sharpest of loops by Hodge around McLaren, whose deft take and feed under pressure showed that the big former Stirling County centre was much more than just a crash-bang-wallop merchant.

So Pool A ended as most folk had anticipated, with the Springboks and Scots in the first two places; Uruguay and Spain followed up in that order.

NEXT
Made in England

NEXT

Official Clothing Sponsors
Leicester Tigers

Hakas and Hits

Mick Cleary

O nly the Tongans didn't raise an eyebrow or two when this pool was formulated. They were just delighted to be anywhere at all in this World Cup, never mind in a group with New Zealand, England and Italy. At least it would give them a Test match against two of the big boys in world rugby – the All Blacks and England – neither of whom had ever played against the poor relations of the Pacific islands.

'We got here through the back door,' said Dave Waterston, Tonga's New Zealand-born coach. 'We had home and away matches in Georgia and South Korea to qualify through the repechage. The hotel in Georgia was like the gulag. And the coach to training had urine stains all over. We don't have any money to speak of. A \$A330,000 grant is all we get from RWC. I had to bribe a local schoolmaster with 50 bags of compost to be able to borrow a playing field for a month for the boys' training. For an impoverished little nation to come here and compete is wonderful. It's the only way we can get to play these teams. Australia and New Zealand have no interest in our position. Their track record proves that. But the boys have done wonderfully. I love them for their guts and their determination.'

Not everyone did. All Black coach John Hart was seething after his side's 45-9 victory over them on the opening weekend before a 22,000 capacity crowd at Ashton Gate in Bristol. Tonga had pegged New Zealand for most of a bruising first half before the All Blacks let rip with three tries in a ten-minute spell after the interval. Jonah Lomu confirmed that he was back in rude health in scoring two tries for New Zealand. Josh Kronfeld, Norm Maxwell and Byron Kelleher scored New Zealand's other tries. Andrew Mehrtens kicked 20 points in all – four conversions and four penalties. But the Tongans left their mark with their aggressive tackling. Too aggressive for Hart's liking. Tongan full back, Siua Taumalolo, who scored all his side's points, was cited and banned for 21 days for dangerous tackling.

England received more of the same treatment when their match, the final one in the group, saw prop Ngalu Taufo'ou sent off for a flying stiff-arm punch on Richard Hill. That dust-up began when England full back Matt

All Black centre Alama Ieremia looks to Josh Kronfeld for support as a flood of Tongan defenders closes in. New Zealand defeated Tonga 45-9, but the going was tough.

The wrong sort of 'big hit'. Tongan prop Ngalu Taufo'ou (1), soon to depart for an early bath, stands over the prone figure of England's Richard Hill, whom he has just felled.

Perry was upended in mid-air by 'Isi Tapueluelu. The Tongan was yellow-carded, as was England prop Phil Vickery, who had decided to exact retribution of his own. That incident occurred in the 35th minute. England led 24-10 and the game was effectively over. They ran out winners by 101-10 in the end, fly half Paul Grayson bagging 36 points to pass the England record set two weeks earlier by Jonny Wilkinson. England scored 13 tries in all. There were two apiece for Will Greenwood, Phil Greening, Jeremy Guscott, Dan Luger and Austin Healey, and one each for Matt Perry, Richard Hill and Matt Dawson. Former Bristol wing Tevita Tiueti scored Tonga's try, converted by Sateki Tu'ipulotu, who also kicked a penalty.

Italy made up the Pool B quartet but were none too happy about finding themselves in such illustrious company – again. They were matched with England and New Zealand at the 1991 World Cup and were in the same group as one or other of them in the two other World Cups. This time around, Italy had qualified through

England's group and had almost caused a major upset by coming close to beating England in the qualifying match at Huddersfield in November 1998. They had a perfectly good try scored by scrum half Alessandro Troncon disallowed. England, thanks to a late try by centre Will Greenwood, ran out 23-15 winners. And yet who do Italy end up having to play again? England.

Still a wonderful sight for rugby lovers. Jeremy Guscott in full flight as he covers the length of the field to score during England's 101-10 destruction of Tonga.

Matt Dawson is joined in celebration by Austin Healey, Danny Grewcock and Phil Vickery after the scrum half had opened England's World Cup try account against Italy.

'It is very difficult to have to do this and play the same team for three consecutive World Cups,' said Italy's captain, No. 8 Massimo Giovanelli. 'You have to ask whether this is ideal or if there might be an economic reason for it. How can it happen, too, that five teams at a global competition have home advantage. Is this fair? Is this right? The RWC can change this if they wanted to because they have changed other things. The conclusion is that they don't want to.'

Giovanelli's fears proved to be on the button. His team were swatted aside in quite ruthless fashion by both England and New Zealand. Their morale, already fragile after a difficult, unrewarding season, was shattered.

England played well to beat Italy 67-7 in the opening match of Pool B in front of a 72,500 full house at Twickenham. England left out Jeremy Guscott in favour of a centre pairing of Phil de Glanville and Will Greenwood and opted for a front row of Jason Leonard, Richard Cockerill and Phil Vickery. England had got themselves in the right frame of mind for this potentially testing first game when expectation was running high.

'The time of Italy being a team to take lightly is gone,' said England captain Martin Johnson. 'It is a big challenge for us.' England rose to it. They were streetwise and pragmatic but also sharp and inventive. Italy clung on by their fingertips in an attempt to keep in the match but were eventually swamped. England did not become frustrated by Italy's attempts to slow the game down. They merely bided their time and waited for the opportune moment. There was a rousing performance from Matt Dawson at scrum half and strong surges down the wings from both Dan Luger and Austin Healey. Jonny Wilkinson at fly half ran the show with splendid shrewdness, mixing his options and resisting the temptation to fling everything wide in an effort to run the Italians ragged. Wilkinson broke the English points-scoring record, passing by two the 30-point mark set by Paul Grayson and Rob Andrew.

The most impressive feature of England's play was their composure. It would have been so easy to snatch at opportunities. But, no. They bided their time, kicked their goals in the early stages and waited for the Italian resistance to fade. 'We wanted to get a buffer early on,' said Martin Johnson. 'So it was important to take the penalty goals when on offer. It paid off. Their interception try didn't unsettle us. It was important just to get points on the board.'

Tonga scrum half Sililo Martens takes on Italy's fly half Diego Dominguez at Welford Road, Leicester. Tonga won dramatically 28-25 to leave Italy facing a whitewash.

The All Blacks wiped out Italy at Huddersfield, scoring 14 tries in their 101-3 victory. Here Italy's Dominguez (10) and Pini, a former Wallaby, struggle to hold Daryl Gibson.

Wilkinson had already kicked four goals by the time Diego Dominguez nipped away for Italy's try in the 25th minute. Matt Dawson had scored a try for England in the tenth minute. England were clearly on top. Two tries within two minutes just before the interval from Richard Hill and Phil de Glanville put England in the driving seat. It took no time at all after the break for England to gain the initiative once more. Matt Perry was put in at the corner by a smart lobbed pass from Austin Healey. The Leicester wing was a key man on the night, popping up all over the field.

Wilkinson's first ever try for England in the 52nd minute owed everything to Healey's electric break from deep and well-placed chip kick ahead. The Italian cover made a hash of reclaiming the ball, and the Newcastle fly half took full advantage. England finished at a gallop, running in three tries in the final 12 minutes, from Dan Luger, Neil Back and Martin Corry, to win 67-7.

It was a very solid showing, but England were not about to be lured into making false claims on their own behalf for their next match against the All Blacks. 'Italy are not in the same league as the guys next week,' said England coach Clive Woodward. 'So let's not get too carried away. We're seeing the benefits of all the time spent together. This was a tricky game for England. The roof was waiting to fall in on us if it hadn't gone well. The boys coped with that.'

And that is more than can be said for Italy. They never recovered. They lost eight days later at Welford Road to Tonga, felled by a dramatic 45-metre dropped goal struck by full back Sateki Tu'ipulotu three minutes into injury time. That gave Tonga a 28-25 victory and meant that Italy were looking at a whitewash. Their final opponents were the All Blacks. Could they salvage any respectability? No, they could not. The All Blacks made hay at the McAlpine Stadium in Huddersfield, breaking through the century of points with Tony Brown's last-minute conversion of Glen Osborne's try, albeit the New Zealander appeared to be in row three of the stands when he touched down in the corner. Osborne had the good grace to admit so. 'I didn't think that I had scored,' he said. 'I stood up to walk back disappointed and I saw that the ref had put his hand up for the try.'

That made the score 99-3. Brown, who already had 36 points to his name, made no mistake with the final conversion. There was a hat-trick of tries for Jeff Wilson, two apiece for Jonah Lomu and Glen Osborne, with Brown, Christian Cullen, Daryl Gibson, Mark Hammett, Dylan Mika, Taine Randell and Scott Robertson weighing in with one try each. Jeff Wilson became New Zealand's all-time leading try scorer, while Lomu beat Rory Underwood's record of 11 tries in World Cup matches.

So, what does that leave in this group? Ah, yes. England against the All Blacks, a minor little skirmish in the World Cup turf war. This game was always going to get top billing in this pool. The winner would have a much easier route through the knockout stages. The loser would have to face an extra match in the play-offs, before heading across the Channel to Paris to face the world champions, South Africa, just four days later. In fact the game's significance extended far beyond that. There was history and hype all rolled up together, the mouthwatering prospect of the most successful outfit in the history of the sport – the All Blacks – against a country that aspired to

Two key players of the England v New Zealand clash meet in battle as Andrew Mehrtens hauls down Lawrence Dallaglio, with a little help from Alama Ieremia.

such status. The All Blacks had won 238 of their 331 Test matches played up to that point, a return of 74.32 per cent. England's tally stood at 55.47 per cent.

Ever since he took office in October 1997, Clive Woodward had cited the World Cup as his target, the tournament which was to be the gauge for his success or his failure. This game would prove to be a critical benchmark. Or would it? The tussle for the psychological edge began early. All Black coach John Hart nudged the stakes upwards by wondering whether England were placing too much emphasis on this game, which, after all, was no more than a group match. 'England have been talking about this match for 12-15 months,' said Hart. 'Clive Woodward has been talking it up and they have put a huge challenge upon themselves. There is far more pressure on them than on us. I do believe you have to be careful about these things. You can think that the match is too big. All eyes in the England camp have been on October 9. The World Cup won't be won or lost then. It will be won or lost on November 6.'

The All Blacks made one change to the side that had beaten Tonga, Craig Dowd coming in on the tight-head for the injured Kees Meeuws. Dowd was winning his 50th cap, although the vast majority of those Tests had seen him bind arms on the opposite side of the scrum. Star wing-

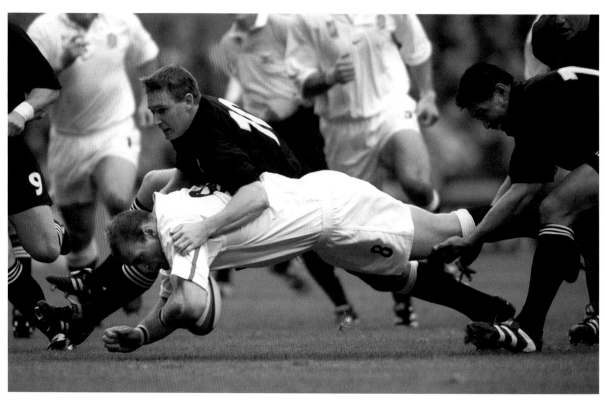

Jeff Wilson looks up after scoring New Zealand's first try against England. There was a hint that the final pass had gone forward, but TV replays seemed to show it was legal.

turned-full back Jeff Wilson was also about to notch a half century of caps.

England, too, made one change to their line-up, Jeremy Guscott reclaiming his position in the centre. Will Greenwood may well have kept his place if his tweaked hamstring had responded to treatment a tad quicker. Greenwood made it to the bench. Guscott, who has seen a bit of action in his time, was delighted to be given the chance of doing battle with the All Blacks. 'If you can't get excited by the thought of playing this lot then you shouldn't be in the game,' said Guscott, who was to win his 64th cap. 'It will be like a massive game of chess out there with each side trying to second guess the other. It will be awesome.'

One other name loomed large in the build-up: bloke by the name of Lomu. He too has done a bit in his time, brief as it has been. How were England going to cope with the destructive force that had blown them apart in the World Cup semi-final four years earlier? 'You don't put seven or eight men on to one of theirs,' said Guscott. 'It just

doesn't work that way.' Perhaps England should have done, for it was once again the big fella' in black that proved to be England's downfall.

The match itself was a gripping contest, full of sound and fury from the first whistle. The daft little spat as to whether England could play their adopted anthem 'Swing Low Sweet Chariot' before the kick-off had the effect of stoking the fires in the crowd. There was a wonderful atmosphere, a buzz of anticipation from all quarters. Several thousand Kiwis made their voices heard. England captain Martin Johnson had made his voice heard during the week. 'We are talking small edges in this one,' said Johnson. 'No one will dominate. It will come down to the fine line. It's up to us to be on the right side of it.'

England did not manage to claim that vital piece of territory for long enough stretches. Every time they set up camp in the land of the self-confident, they were turfed out

Phil de Glanville is rewarded for chasing Jeremy Guscott's kick ahead and manages to touch down for England's try, despite the close attention of All Black Tana Umaga.

to the other side of the dividing line. New Zealand consistently had the edge that Johnson was talking about. England had the opportunity to gain a foothold, only to make mistakes at the critical moments. Jonny Wilkinson had a flawed afternoon with the boot, missing two penalties within the first 25 minutes. Four kicks went wide in all. Richard Cockerill fluffed three throws to the line out, while the statistics show that England turned over the ball 12 times. Even so, they still had a huge amount of ball to play with. They won 73 rucks to New Zealand's 21. They also won the ball 80 times in open play compared with 24 by the All Blacks. 'I'd be surprised if one of my sides came up with stats like that,' said Hart.

And why did England come up with figures like that? They lost control of both ball and territory at key times. They may have seemed like minor infringements at times, such as when Cockerill drove into Johnson early in the game to concede a scrum for accidental offside. But, as Johnson had predicted, the team that doesn't make those sorts of mistakes is the team that will invariably come out on top. New Zealand were more composed. They believed

in themselves more profoundly than England and did not panic or snatch at the moment. Their pack came together wonderfully on the day, belying their status. Craig Dowd was a masterful influence on the loose-head, Robin Brooke a rallying point for the forwards.

England had their own heroes. Lawrence Dallaglio was once again a driving force all over the field, while Matt Perry at full back was a calm presence. But England had no one to match two key All Black figures – fly half Andrew Mehrtens and open-side flanker Josh Kronfeld. Between them they kept England on the back foot. Mehrtens mixed his bag with cunning, sometimes rolling kicks behind the defence, other times sticking it in the air. Kronfeld gave one of the great exhibitions of open-side play and was responsible for Jonny Wilkinson having such a nervy afternoon. He lived in Wilkinson's face, forcing him to rush and to make wrong decisions. Kronfeld also succeeded in slowing down much of England's ball.

And then there was Lomu. Would New Zealand have won without him? Probably, for they were superior in the most important phases of the game. With him, the result swung dramatically their way as the clock approached the hour mark. England had just clawed their way back to 16-16 and Twickenham was jumping.

Mehrtens had opened the scoring with a penalty after 11 minutes. Five minutes later Jeff Wilson was on hand to take a pop pass out of the tackle from Tana Umaga to squeeze in at the corner. Mehrtens converted. New Zealand led 13-3 at the interval, an advantage which Mehrtens soon increased with his third penalty of the afternoon two minutes after the break. England were not about to roll over meekly. A slithered kick through by Jeremy Guscott in the 48th minute was chased by Matt Perry and New Zealand's Justin Marshall. Both of them missed the ball, but Phil de Glanville didn't. The England centre got the touchdown by planting the ball against the base of the posts. The conversion and a penalty five minutes later by Wilkinson brought the scores level.

Could England do it? Could they ride the wave? No. They were brought crashing back to earth by Jonah Lomu. The winger received a long pass from Mehrtens – which looked forward – some 55 metres from goal. He set off. Four England white shirts stood between him and the line. Guscott, Healey, Dawson and Luger all fell by the wayside. Lomu had scored another sensational try. It was

wonderful theatre. The conversion made the scoreline 23-16 and a chill gripped English hearts. New Zealand sealed England's fate with a try from Byron Kelleher 11 minutes from time. Healey was swamped by Reuben Thorne and Craig Dowd, and the ball popped out for substitute Kelleher to scamper to the line.

It was a terrific performance by the All Blacks, to have faced up to the opposition and their own supposed points of weakness. 'It ranks right up there with the best,' said Hart. England got the balance of their game wrong, kicking when they should have run, and running when they ought to have kicked. Three pieces of possession went skywards in the first 90 seconds. 'If we'd gone out of the competition that way then I'd never have spoken to the players again,' said Clive Woodward a few days later.

England hadn't gone out of the competition. The road ahead, though, now looked more like an assault course.

Jonah Lomu steps out as Matt Dawson (hidden) closes in. The big man stunned England with a breathtaking long-range solo try just after the home side had drawn level.

Now even more flights to the world from your local airport.

Worth a try.

From all over the UK, to all over the world. **KLM** uk

Pool of Certainty?

Alastair Hignell

Simon Raiwalui of Fiji (left) and Namibia's Heino Senekal compete in the line out in the Pool C opener at Béziers. Senekal went on to score his country's first World Cup try.

When the Rugby World Cup groupings were first announced, Pool C seemed the least exciting. All the other groups had at least one mouthwatering clash, while Pool D, where an underconfident Wales were to host the strong-scrummaging Argentinians, the dangerous Samoans and the Kiwi-bolstered Japanese, was dubbed the 'Pool of Death'. Pool C was the 'Pool of Certainty', with double Grand Slam champions France expected to stroll past ageing Canada and underperforming Fiji, with 'minnows' Namibia a distant fourth.

Then France fell apart. A dismal Five Nations, including home defeats by Wales and Scotland, was followed by a disastrous tour to the southern hemisphere and an August defeat by Wales in Cardiff. Injuries proliferated, while rumours of dissension within the squad were rife. Canada, meanwhile, were competitive against both England and Wales, and Fiji, under the astute guidance of Brad Johnstone, at last seemed to be transferring their extraordinary world-beating sevens talents to the 15-man game. The 'Pool of Certainty' had all the potential to turn into the 'Pool of Chaos'. In the event, 'C' was to stand for Competitive. The matches between France, Fiji and Canada could have gone either way, while those against the hapless Namibians were guided by the need to rack up as many points as possible in case of a top-of-the-table tie.

Fiji were the first to take on the southern Africans, on the opening day of the tournament. The French Rugby Federation's policy of staging their matches in pairs away from the Stade de France in Paris meant that even for a match such as this the Stade Meditérranée at Béziers welcomed 10,000 fans. The Fijians, whose happy demeanour and determination to stay away from the larger, more impersonal centres of population had already gained them a legion of admirers, made even more friends with a sparkling nine-try extravaganza. Wing Fero

Fiji full back Alfred Uluinayau takes on Namibia's Arthur Samuelson. There were no points at Béziers for the Fijian, but he scored a stunning try against France at Toulouse.

Lasagavibau scored two of them, the first to overhaul a penalty from Namibia's full back-turned-wing Leandre van Dyk. And with former Leicester outside half Waisale Serevi in superlative kicking form – he ended with 11 successes from 12 shots at goal – the Fijians were 43-6 up at half-time and coasting.

After 12 minutes of the second half, the honour of scoring Namibia's first ever World Cup try fell to Heino Senekal, and though Mario Jacobs added a second after 21 minutes, Fijian No. 8 Alivereti Mocelutu had already seen his team past the 50-point mark, and captain Greg Smith and scrum half Jacob Rauluni were to follow him onto the scoresheet. Fiji, who had failed to win a match in RWC 1995 after failing to qualify in 1991, had hit the ground running in RWC 1999.

Canada, as quarter-finalists in 1991 and honourable third-best in the 1995 'Group of Death' behind South Africa and Australia, had even loftier ambitions. Despite

a disappointing Pacific Rim tournament, they had once again assembled a rugged and durable outfit. In captain and outside half Gareth Rees, they had the only player to appear in all four World Cups. As one of the very few professionals in the Canadian outfit he felt his team had made great strides in August internationals against Wales and England. He felt they could improve on their 1991 showing. 'I honestly believe we can beat France on their own soil,' he said in the run-up to the first match. 'We gave them a real fright when we were last here, eight years ago, and I think that this Canadian side is every bit as good as its predecessor. France appear to have slipped a bit and playing them first I think we have a great chance to cause an upset before they can get into their stride.'

Rees was so nearly right. The captain himself booted Canada into a 3-0 lead in just the second minute of the match, and his conversion of scrum half Morgan Williams' outstanding solo try again gave the visitors the lead after Richard Dourthe had kicked a penalty and fellow centre Stephane Glas had raced over for an unconverted try. Dourthe's second penalty restored the French lead, but when Rees, who had passed a late fitness test on his troublesome right leg, was hurt in the run-up to France's second try, scored by Olivier Magne in the last minute of the first half, Canada's hopes went with their playmaker.

But not, however, before Williams had scored his second superb try, from a quickly taken tapped penalty, and Bobby Ross had converted to narrow the gap to a single point. But an injury to French full back Ugo Mola forced a tactical rethink: Christophe Lamaison came on at outside half, with Thomas Castaignède moving to full back; France began to play a much tighter game. Within minutes Castaignède himself was driven over from close range by his pack, and Dourthe had added his third penalty. Although Ross pulled three points back, France had by now established control. Although they continued to commit unforced errors there was a better shape and a greater urgency to their game. It was still a rare bout of fluent interpassing which gave substitute Emile Ntamack a try with just three minutes to go. France were home and dry, but far from convincing.

The relief in the French camp was almost tangible. Coach Jean-Claude Skrela paid tribute to the opposition – 'we found Canada an immense problem' – and to his team's defence – 'our tackling was superb'. But he was still critical of his own players – 'we made errors...lacked concentration...and gave away two easy tries...' Captain Raphael Ibañez, however, put a different spin on it: 'The lapses in concentration were because of the huge task of coming back from such a bad period of results for us and it was the first match in the competition. We adapted to situations. We have no injuries and I am happy.'

The French captain had no idea what a hostage to fortune he was giving. Castaignède was to tear a thigh muscle in training and take his leave of the tournament; Thomas Lièvremont and Stephane Glas were to be injured in the next match against Namibia; and by the third pool game, against Fiji, scrum half Pierre Mignoni had bowed out of the tournament for good.

The 22-year-old from Toulon did, however, score France's first try against Namibia. As against Canada, though, France were made to struggle early on by a gutsy and committed Namibian team. In front of 34,000 fans at the Stade Lescure in Bordeaux, the Africans tore into their hosts from the start and even had the temerity to be

French flanker Olivier Magne on the charge in France's opening game, against Canada at Béziers. Magne contributed France's second try, on the stroke of half-time.

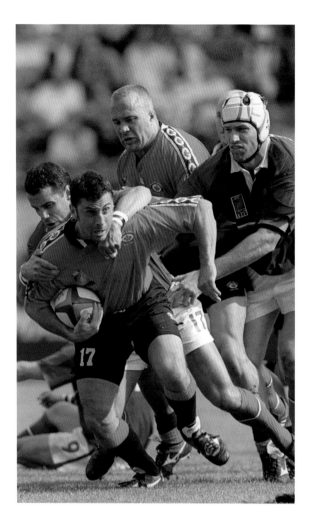

another late touchdown from Ntamack and a flurry of late substitutions, including that of captain Ibañez with a quarter of an hour still to play, was that.

Again, the French management was far from happy. Again, the differing explanations of captain and coach suggested tension behind the scenes. Skrela was blunt: 'We were not vigorous enough in our approach and we need to be a lot sharper. We made too many errors and the main reason for this was that our backs were running too far without support and we gave away too many penalties.' Ibañez was more specific: 'Our backs were too proud to adapt against the Namibian strong defence and we were too slow to release the ball from the scrums and the mauls.' France, though, had two wins, however unconvincing, from two games. Canada, on the other hand, faced the opposite scenario. Before their opening game against France, they had realistic hopes of victory and a position at the top of the pool. Now they faced Fiji knowing that a quarter-final place depended on it.

Once again captain Gareth Rees patched up his weary body. Once again he inspired his team to near-heroics. With a quarter of an hour gone, Canada led 10-0. They had scored a penalty try after just five minutes, when

Replacement v replacement, as France's Christophe Lamaison, on for full back Ugo Mola, tackles Canada's Bobby Ross, on for the injured Gareth Rees.

on level terms after 20 minutes. With Dourthe swapping penalties with van Dyk after converting Mignoni's try, France, playing as carelessly as they had for long periods against Canada, were rocked back on their heels when Namibian wing Arthur Samuelson latched on to a pass from centre Francois van Rensburg to score under the posts and make van Dyk's conversion a formality.

Dourthe added a couple more penalties – to van Dyk's one – to restore the French lead, but for the second match running France were indebted to a score on the stroke of half-time, this one falling to Philippe Bernat-Salles, to calm their nerves. It didn't spare their blushes, however. The fans in Bordeaux booed their team off the pitch at the interval and were only slightly mollified by a second-half hat-trick from full back Ugo Mola. That, apart from

Thomas Castaignède began at fly half against Canada, moving to full back when Lamaison was introduced after 55 minutes. A training injury then ended his World Cup.

Emile Ntamack crosses for France in the 70th minute against Namibia. Despite six tries and a 43-12 scoreline, the French were far from convincing.

referee Ed Morrison ruled obstruction against Fiji, and in the process spared the blushes of Canadian forwards Mike James and Rod Snow, who, with the line at their mercy and with no Fijian in sight, had both failed to ground the ball. With half an hour gone, they were 16-5 up, with Rees having added a couple of penalties and a dropped goal to his earlier conversion, while all Fiji could manage was a well-worked try for centre Viliame Satala. By half-time, however, Canada were behind. Outside half Nicky Little, preferred to Serevi for this match, converted a penalty try, again awarded for obstruction, as well as adding the two points when Satala skated over for his second touchdown, before adding an injury-time penalty for good measure.

Little's hot streak continued at the start of the second half, though his dropped goal after two minutes was matched by Rees' third penalty. The match only went beyond Canada's reach, however, when former Leicester

wing Marika Vunibaka scored a stunning individual try from a kick ahead, for Little to convert. Rees and Little swapped two more penalties apiece as Fiji coasted home. The only sour note was the injury-time dismissal of Vunibaka for a head-butt on Canadian centre Kyle Nichols. The consequences for Vunibaka for a moment's craziness were negligible. A disciplinary tribunal ruled that the sending-off was punishment itself and freed him to play in Fiji's next game.

For Canada, on the other hand, the consequences of a second successive defeat were immense. The players had gone into the tournament fully aware that for rugby to prosper in their country a series of eye-catching and headline-making victories was imperative. At least with 42 points in the bag and a game against Namibia to come they felt they still had a chance of progressing through to the knockout stages as the best of the third-placed teams. That was until they heard the news of Samoa's defeat of Wales. That result meant that, with Argentina likely to beat Japan in the final group game in Pool D, a minimum of eight match points (three points were awarded for a win, one for a defeat) would be needed to qualify for the quarter-final play-offs. Canada had two, and a maximum possible of five. Nevertheless, they piled into the hapless Namibians from the start of their match in Toulouse, a try from scrum half Williams, his third of the tournament, soon wiping out van Dyk's opening penalty, and three more – to Nichols, Al Charron and Rod Snow – following before the break. Rees converted all four and added a penalty, while Namibia could manage only another three points from the boot of van Dyk.

His right leg heavily strapped, Gareth Rees, Canada's fly half and captain, hangs on to Fiji's Viliame Satala. Rees ended RWC 1999 with a 100 per cent goal-kicking record.

Despite having flanker Dan Baugh sent off for stamping early in the second half – to receive a 28-day ban – Canada ran in another five tries after the break. Nichols, Ross, Stanley (2) and Snow were the scorers, and Rees converted all five and added two penalties for a match haul of 27 points. In the immediate aftermath of Baugh's dismissal, Namibian skipper Quinn Hough touched down for an unconverted try.

Namibia, then, were definitely on the next plane home, their first ever World Cup finals ending winless. Nevertheless, coach Rudy Joubert was in ebullient mood in considering his team's campaign as a whole. 'The high point of our World Cup was against France, when we could see how close to victory we were. Against Canada and Fiji we folded, because, under pressure, our players are not used to making quick decisions.' Nevertheless, he predicted bright futures in the game for Hough, Sean Furter his young No. 8, and van Dyk, before firing one last parting shot on the differences between the haves and the have-nots of the game. 'It is very hard to train players in

Fiji wing Marika Vunibaka on his way to score a brilliant try to extinguish Canada's hopes at Bordeaux. Ten minutes later Vunibaka had gone from hero to villain.

just three months, and I think they have done more than anyone can have expected them to achieve. But when they are only on 100 francs a day expenses it is difficult to understand in the modern world of professional rugby.'

Canada's amateurs had, perhaps, just as much cause to complain. Their 1991 campaign had been conducted entirely in France, away from what they considered the English-speaking mainstream of the tournament. Yet in 1999, here they were again, and without the compensation that success can bring. Their exit from the tournament was confirmed when, as expected, Argentina beat Japan, preventing a back-door entry into the quarter-final play-offs.

For coach Pat Parfrey, the final match victory against Namibia was enough to restore his team's pride. 'We set out to show our supporters and the world what Canadian rugby is capable of. The win has focused Canadian rugby.' It also marked the end of the line for Gareth Rees. The only man to have played in all pool matches in all four World Cups had hauled himself through this tournament. His heavily strapped right leg didn't inhibit his goal-kicking, though. His success rate – 11 conversions and nine penalties from 20 kicks in three matches – may, like

Marika Vunibaka head butts Canada centre Kyle Nichols in the final moments of the game. Vunibaka was dismissed but received no further punishment.

France's Richard Dourthe and Emile Ntamack (12), playing alongside one another in the centre, battle for the ball with Fiji's full back, Alfred Uluinayau (15).

his appearance record, be matched, but it will never be beaten. It was a fitting way for one of the game's great characters to step down from the international stage, as a player at least. 'I look forward to being involved in Canadian rugby in some ways,' he offered at the team's closing media conference, before paying his dues, with typical modesty, to the sport he has graced since bursting on to the scene as a Harrow schoolboy to play for Wasps in the 1986 John Player Special Cup final. 'I wouldn't be here today if it wasn't for rugby.'

Which left two unbeaten teams to contest one automatic quarter-final place. Whoever won the last group game between France and Fiji in Toulouse would not only be guaranteed a week's rest before their next game, in Dublin, but would also know that between them and a place in the last four was, in all probability, workmanlike but limited and underconfident Ireland. The

losers, however, would have to travel to Twickenham to face an England side that, despite losing to the All Blacks, had run in 184 points and 22 tries in three pool games.

The preparations of the two teams couldn't have contrasted more strongly. The Fijians, buoyed by the bright sunshine and warm hospitality in the south of France, had been relaxed and smiling. On the field, their dazzling style had won them admirers wherever they went. Off it, their good humour and willingness to mix with the locals had won them countless friends – the 'Fiji Pétanque Championships', for example, featured the Teletubbies (tight forwards), Last There (loose forwards), A Few Good Men (half backs), and Finishers (outside backs).

The French, meanwhile, appeared sullen, divided and riddled with injury. When Mignoni was forced to pull out of the tournament, the selectors turned back to Colomiers scrum half Fabien Galthié, a veteran of the 1991 campaign. The decision may have been right on rugby grounds, but French journalists were not slow to point out that when Galthié had been dropped after the summer tour, he declared that in future he wouldn't cross the road to talk to national coach Jean-Claude Skrela. Yet here they were, forced by circumstance to work together again.

It was Stephane Castaignède, however, who started against Fiji, with Galthié on the bench. A sun-baked crowd of some 40,000 saw France start the stronger. Although Richard Dourthe's opening penalty was swiftly cancelled out by a strike from Nicky Little, a close-range drive from a line out saw No. 8 Christophe Juillet power over for a try. Dourthe's conversion and another penalty left the half-time score at 13-3, although how it stayed at that total only Paddy O'Brien knew. The New Zealand referee first of all awarded a try to French wing Christophe Dominici, then disallowed it because he said he'd forgotten that Christophe Lamaison had indicated his intention to kick at goal. Then he disallowed a Fijian try by flanker Setareki Tawake, ruling that Fiji had knocked the ball on when in fact it was French full back Mola who had lost possession in a tackle.

O'Brien's conduct during the second half when France had a series of scrums on the Fijian line was equally inexplicable. Fiji by this time had raced into a 19-13 lead, with Little adding two more penalties and converting a stunning long-range try from Alfred Uluinayau. Now, in a ten-minute period France had nine set scrums, some of

them taken as penalty options. At two of them O'Brien punished Fiji props Joe Veitayaki and Dan Rouse with yellow cards. While many other referees might have awarded a penalty try earlier, O'Brien did so at a scrum where it seemed that France, rather than Fiji, were committing an offence. The award sapped the life out of Fiji. A late long-range penalty from Christophe Lamaison and an injury-time try from Christophe Dominici, after a suspiciously forward final pass, merely put a gloss on the scoreboard. France, somehow, had earned themselves a week off. Fiji had the dubious pleasure of heading to Twickenham for a quarter-final play-off.

In the end, then, the 'Pool of Chaos' was predictable enough. France won all their matches to top the group. Namibia lost all theirs. The Fijians' flair proved too much for the Canadians' discipline. Yet the bare facts don't tell the whole story. This group saw more than its fair share of keenly contested matches. Each team, even Namibia in the first half against France, had its day in the sun. The fans, turning out in far greater numbers than in Scotland and Ireland, certainly got their money's worth.

Christophe Dominici, the French left wing, gratefully grounds the ball for his last-gasp try in France's victory over Fiji in the group decider at Toulouse.

Pool D. 'D' as in Death, except that it turned out to be 'D' for Drama. And as does any drama, it began with the raising of the curtain – the Opening Ceremony in Cardiff, laid on by the host nation, Wales. 'Host nation' was a peculiar phrase bearing in mind that the competition was spread around five countries, but the first and last games were to be played at the Millennium Stadium, so Wales took it upon themselves to welcome everybody to the party. Since, even under Graham Henry, it was unlikely that they would be there for the final – one of the advantages bestowed upon the 'host nation' was that they would have to travel to Twickenham for their semi-final – Wales decided to give it the full works on Day One. They would make everybody aware of the Welshness of the tournament, just before Match Two kicked off in that eisteddfod hot-spot of the south, Béziers, where Fiji would play Namibia.

What the Welsh in Wales came up with was very...Welsh. Catatonia sang how great it was to be Welsh, Max Boyce said how much the Good Lord enjoyed watching Wales play, and the capacity crowd, almost all of them Welsh, felt that this was a World Cup moment that made you proud to be Welsh. Meanwhile, the rest of the world tried not to snigger. The drama was already melodramatic. Unfortunately, as the crowd swayed and wept, the brand new Millennium Stadium started to fall to bits, a metal bolt rolling off the roof and breaking the arm of a passing fan. Luckily – inevitably, given the composition of the throng – she happened to be Welsh and had the good grace to wait until Monday before threatening to sue. It was all too dripping in emotion to be of any use to the Welsh players who had to play against Argentina. The Quinnell brothers, who have been around a bit, went out to have a look at the myriad squares of turf that make up the playing surface of their new home and went back to the changing room speechless at the intensity of the fanaticism up above. Scott Gibbs, who has been around even longer and been to even more places, shed a tear during the anthems.

Wales played patchily. Part of the trouble was that they were playing against a side they had beaten three times already in the previous ten months; another part

Colin Charvis turns after scoring Wales' first try against Argentina. The Wales flanker was later cited for a tussle with the Pumas' Roberto Grau and banned for two matches.

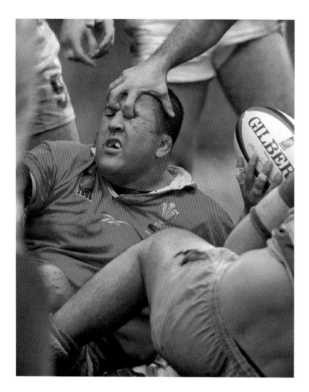

Wales hooker Garin Jenkins seems to have his eyes gouged by an Argentinian player. It proved impossible to identify whose hand was at work, and no one was punished.

was that Scott Gibbs, the focus of so many midfield moves, was not only emotionally a little high but also virally a touch low. The Welsh held the threat of the Puma scrummage at bay but did not really gel beyond that. They had one purple patch around half-time, however, which allowed them to build up a healthy lead. Mark Taylor and Colin Charvis scored tries, both converted by Neil Jenkins, and Wales were 23-9 up. And all that happened from then until the end of the game was that Gonzalo Quesada kept nibbling away at the deficit with penalties, the Argentinian fly half ending the afternoon with six in all.

The crowd, drained by the Opening Ceremony, was muted throughout the match, although there was a huge sigh when Wales survived a line out on their own try line late in the second half. A converted try by the Pumas at that moment and the great welcome would have become the great wailing. There was one other thing: the entrance of Jason Jones-Hughes as a replacement for the off-colour Scott Gibbs. Jason of Sydney, New South Wales, the son of Gwyn from Colwyn Bay, old North Wales, was the latest and most contentious of the catches from the other side of the world. Wales already had Brett Sinkinson and

Shane Howarth from New Zealand, while Peter Rogers had come back via a long spell in South Africa. But Jones-Hughes had been pinched directly from the Australian development system. His tackling and distribution in the 20 minutes he played showed why Graham Henry had been so keen to bring him home to the land of his father.

The question of eligibility was soon to be raised again, but not because of nationality. Colin Charvis would be banned from appearing in the next two games, cited by the match commissioner following a tussle with Roberto Grau. The Argentinian prop had been shown the yellow card by referee Paddy O'Brien but received an additional sanction of a three-week suspension. Charvis received two. In an attempt to clean up the game's image, Rugby World Cup were on the look-out for any nonsense. If the game was to travel to new fields – and German distaste for the unwholesome aspects of rugby was cited as the obstacle to progress – it needed to have its act cleaned up, and the video match commissioner was just the person to do it. Charvis and Grau had hardly waged biological warfare on each other. They had wrestled and flailed with a couple of punches. If three- and two-week bans were to be handed out for such peccadilloes, what would happen if something more extreme happened?

Without wishing to suggest that Brendan Reidy did anything particularly heinous either in the next game in Pool D, between Samoa and Japan, it did seem that when he was cited for punching he would at least receive some sort of ban. But no, Reidy escaped, and Charvis, who lodged an appeal on the basis that the playing field did not seem very level on this new issue of violence, had his ban upheld. Perhaps Charvis was not helped by the fact that he became an overnight cause célèbre. T-shirts were printed: 'Free Colin Charvis'. Rugby World Cup and their earnest video match commissioners cannot have been best amused, especially when Gareth Thomas raised his red shirt in the act of scoring a try in the next Welsh game against Japan to reveal the said white T-shirt. It was an echo of Robbie Fowler, the Liverpool footballer, raising his shirt at Anfield to reveal his support for the striking Liverpool dockers: political awareness among sports people, with a nice touch of humour. But as the International Rugby Board always used to say when allowing Lions teams to travel to South Africa in the boycott years, politics and sport do not mix.

On the receiving end of both the Reidy punch and the Thomas try were Japan. Much had been expected of them,

Two former All Blacks who returned to their roots: Samoa's Va'aiga Tuigamala, playing at centre, runs at the Japan defence with fly half Stephen Bachop in close support.

reinforced as they now were by a posse of Kiwis: Graeme Bachop, Greg Smith, Jamie Joseph and Andrew McCormick. They arrived as champions of the Pacific Rim and carried the hopes of all those looking for a breakthrough by a side not belonging to the Big Eight cartel of the countries who competed in the Five Nations and Tri-Nations championships.

Unfortunately, for all their added bulk, what Japan needed most on their first outing was kind weather and a good playing surface, so that their handling skills could be revealed. Their Kiwi weight was but a welcome variation on the speed and flow of the traditional Japanese game. In Wrexham on the day they played Samoa it belted down with rain. The same old problems as always knocked Japan backwards. Unable to duck and weave, they were flattened by the big Samoan tacklers. If a country was to

use the World Cup as a stage on which to mount a challenge on the global order, it seemed more likely that it would be Manu Samoa rather than Japan.

But who were we to think that such a challenge was new? Samoa had been to the quarter-finals in the previous two World Cups, which put them already on a pedestal above Wales, whose exploits in 1991 and 1995 were not read out to the crowd at the Opening Ceremony. Now, by beating Japan comprehensively, it seemed Samoa were on their way to a third successive quarter-final. In fact, this time they were stronger than ever, for they had reinforcements of their own. Stephen Bachop, brother of Japan's Graeme, had also played for the New Zealand All

Blacks. And outside him was the mighty Va'aiga Tuigamala, another ex-All Black, also ex-Rugby League, and, with Newcastle, still one of the outstanding personalities of the Premiership club scene in England.

Japan did not recover from that opening experience in North Wales. They went south to Cardiff to face Wales. They began well enough, one try by wing Daisuke Ohata, who scorched over the perfect playing surface – and exposed what Graham Henry had always felt might be his team's weak spot: raw speed – showing what might one day be, but Japan thereafter never truly extended their opponents. The Welsh by way of contrast were much more relaxed – almost too relaxed at times – and scored 38

One of the most exciting backs of the tournament was Daisuke Ohata of Japan, seen here in action against Samoa. His electric pace on the wing made him a constant menace.

points without reply in the second half in a spate of try-scoring that included the Gareth Thomas T-shirt diversion. The only person who confessed to being tense was Neil Jenkins. The outside half was continually being reminded – 'even by the bloke who brings on the sand,' said Wales' prolific kicker – that leading up to the Japan game he stood only 20 points short of Michael Lynagh's world record of 911 points in international rugby. 'It's doing my head in a little bit, to be honest,' Jenkins added.

Jenkins missed a couple of easy kicks, but by the end of the afternoon he had scored 19 points and now stood equal with the great Australian. The two had played in the same number of Tests – 72 – but Jenkins had never known, until recently in the age of Graham Henry, what it was like to play in a successful side. He had accumulated his points the hard way, and he was still two years short of his 30th birthday.

Gareth Thomas raises his Wales jersey to reveal his 'Free Colin Charvis' T-shirt after scoring against Japan. The authorities were unmoved – Charvis served his term.

Lunchtime the next day. Samoa against Argentina at Stradey Park, Llanelli. Maybe this was why the citing commissioners had been so keen to make their mark early. This had the potential to be explosive: the Puma scrummage and the ferocious Samoan tacklers. The rain would serve only as a fuel for the sparks of contact. It turned out to be well disciplined. The commissioner hardly had call to reach for his replay button. Mauricio Reggiardo was put to the test by Junior Paramore to see if his head was properly secured to his shoulders, but the Puma prop shrugged and put his head back in the next scrummage; which was precisely where all the theories about who would lead the charge on the old order were put through the shredder – just like the Samoan scrummage.

Argentina found themselves 3-16 adrift at half-time. They had squandered a few opportunities and were beginning to look very ragged. Given a recent history of

Pumas Ignacio Fernandez Lobbe (left) and Alejandro Allub celebrate Allub's 70th-minute try against Samoa. Argentina wiped out a 16-point half-time deficit to triumph 32-16.

The record at last! Neil Jenkins converts the first of Wales' two penalty tries against Samoa to move to 913 points and become the highest points scorer in international rugby.

Below: A close-run thing. Wales right wing Gareth Thomas sneaks in at the corner to register his 18th-minute try for Wales against Samoa.

strife in the rugby politics of the Pumas, it seemed that they were on their way out. But coach Alex Wyllie – who was 'new-old' in that he'd been acting as a consultant for years but now found himself in sole charge – must have issued a few stern reminders at half-time in his inimical grizzly-avuncular way. Anyway, in the second half the Pumas were transformed, and the Samoans found themselves in retreat at the scrummage and under severe pressure all around the park. Little Agustin Pichot at scrum half drove his forwards on. Second-row Alejandro Allub scored a try. Gonzalo Quesada from outside half dropped a goal and kicked eight penalties. He took an eternity to brace himself for each kick, but 14 penalties in two games spoke for themselves. Argentina scored 29 points in the second half; Samoa added none to their first half 16. Suddenly the complexion of Pool D had changed again. Now it seemed that Argentina would qualify as runners-up. All they had to do was beat Japan in the final

It's all over! Samoa celebrate the reprise of their 1991 World Cup victory over Wales. Samoa's win threw the pool into disarray. Who would play in the next stage, and where?

game and they would go through behind Wales, who would surely beat the Samoans.

If England v New Zealand set the standard for quality play, Wales v Samoa was the most dramatic game of the World Cup so far. Neil Jenkins was still the centre of attention, gaining his 73rd cap and overtaking the individual appearance record set by Ieuan Evans. One more point and he would have that points-scoring record to himself, too. Around him Wales were not quite at full strength. They were still without the suspended Colin Charvis and the injured Craig Quinnell, who was suffering from what his coach called 'a multitude of bumps and bruises'. Perhaps Wales might not be able to squeeze the energy out of the Samoans up front as they had hoped. But that was still the area where they could apply the most pressure. The game, however, was anything but tight. Samoa took an early lead through the boot of Silao Leaega, another to make the art of goal-kicking seem absurdly easy, but soon the maestro himself was lining up his first penalty. Everybody was poised to burst into applause for the Jenkins outright record. But the kick hit

a post and before the crowd had finished its good-natured groan the Samoans were counterattacking with a movement that nearly led to a try at the other end of the field. And that was to be the pattern of the game. Appearances were utterly deceptive. Wales were on top up front. They scored a penalty try whose conversion gave Jenkins his record, were given the benefit of the doubt when Gareth Thomas scored tight against the corner flag, and scored a second penalty try in the second half.

But all around these Welsh moments the Samoans revelled in theirs. They scored five tries, two of them beautifully crafted, three of them gifts from their opponents. Wales threw into a line out on their own line, and Samoa scored. Wales tried a back-row move; Stephen Bachop ran away for the try. Neil Jenkins of all people tried to launch his threequarters, and Pat Lam intercepted for a runaway score. Star performers like Scott Quinnell, Pat Lam's opposite number, had games to forget. Wales had two scrummage opportunities near the Samoan try line to complete either a hat-trick of penalty tries or blast over from short range. A draw could be salvaged. Both came to nothing. Instead, the abiding memory was of the mighty Va'aiga Tuigamala coming off his wing to take Garin Jenkins man and ball. The mighty Samoan tacklers would be seen yet in the World Cup.

Wales' ten-game sequence of victories had come to an end. Samoa simply said, 'What's the big deal? We beat Wales. We always do.' It was a fact that Samoa had beaten Wales in their previous two encounters – in 1991 in the World Cup in Cardiff and three years later in Apia, the Samoan capital. Samoa did not seem particularly bothered by the result and it seemed that even for Wales the defeat would not be too injurious. They had not played

well in the World Cup. Perhaps this was the jolt they needed. The reassuring thing was that they were not in danger of failing to qualify.

But where would they finish? The mathematics of Pool D suddenly had the computers of the land smoking. Samoa and Wales had each won twice, and if Argentina beat Japan it would mean that three teams would qualify from the pool. The winners would have a week's rest and go straight to the quarter-finals, against Australia in Cardiff. The runners-up would have to play in the midweek play-offs, against Scotland at Murrayfield. The third-best – out of all the groups, that is – would go to Lens in northern France to play Ireland in the play-offs.

Strangely enough, this last option – Ireland in Lens, followed by France in Dublin – seemed the best way forward, although it was not available to Wales. They could only be first or second. Argentina had to score 69 points against Japan to head the pool. If the Pumas won by scoring fewer points, Wales would head the group and

Japan had pace to burn on both flanks. Here left wing Pat Tuidrake takes on Argentinian full back Ignacio Corletto at Cardiff. Tuidrake's speed twin Ohata is in support.

No way through here. Argentinian captain Lisandro Arbizu puts in a crunching tackle on his Japanese counterpart, Andrew McCormick, formerly of Canterbury, New Zealand.

Samoa would be second. If Argentina lost, Samoa would be pool winners and Wales second.

Applause charts were printed, so the Welsh public would know who to support at which stage of the final game in Cardiff between Japan and Argentina. Maybe even Japan could qualify if they rattled up a quick ton. What would happen if the match were a draw? It was all so confusing that the public, for the first time in Wales, stayed away. The Millennium Stadium on that Saturday night was not at full capacity. Ticket prices that had been reduced for this supposedly dead-rubber game – before Wales played Samoa – in an attempt to encourage people to watch were raised again in the light of the Welsh defeat. It simply added to the confusion.

The game itself was not confusing. Japan made it clear from the outset that they were not going to roll over and let the Pumas stroll to 70 points, and Argentina set about the simpler task of merely winning the game. Laboriously and effectively Gonzalo Quesada kicked his penalties, adding another seven to his tally and making him another World Cup statistic. His points represented 80 per cent of the Pumas' entire tally in the group stage. At least on this final evening in Cardiff his efforts were complemented by two tries from Agustin Pichot and Diego Albanese. It was a satisfactory end to the Argentinian campaign, for now they would head off to France to face Ireland on neutral soil. Wales would have home advantage and a rest but would have to face Australia, while Samoa would have to face Scotland in Edinburgh.

A satisfactory conclusion; an end that had not been predicted when the tournament kicked off on the same stage a fortnight earlier. But a quiet end nevertheless; a soft fall of the curtain on the pool that had provided the only sustained bursts of dramatic action in the opening phase of the World Cup.

Glenfiddich.

In a league of its own and the world's favourite single malt whisky

Over a 100 years since the first Glenfiddich ran from its stills, the Glenfiddich Distillery remains faithful to its traditional methods of whisky production, ensuring that the unique character of Glenfiddich is not compromised in any way.

For the maximum enjoyment, drink Glenfiddich neat or cut with a little water or ice.

Of David and Goliath

Sean Diffley

US back-row forward Richard Tardits attempts to gather a loose ball as Ireland's Paddy Johns and David Humphreys look on during the Pool E opener at Lansdowne Road.

When Ireland beat Australia for the first time, at Lansdowne Road in 1958, the veteran centre Noel Henderson – a brother-in-law of Jack Kyle – trundled half the length of the field to score the match-winning try. An ancient press photographer named George Leitch claimed that he ran alongside Henderson and was still in plenty of time at the Havelock Square end to take his picture of the score. Noel – and George – dined out on that one for years.

That other noted Irish try at Lansdowne against Australia, the 1991 World Cup one by Gordon Hamilton, was certainly much more of Formula One speed. Any galloping photographer would have been left miles behind. Even, and you can check the video, David Campese gave up the chase. And Hamilton's try was adjudged the try of the tournament and received the Famous Grouse Award.

I suppose the only real similarity between the Henderson try and the Hamilton one is that they were both scored at the Havelock Square end of the ground. Even though it's eight years since that close shave for the Aussies in Dublin, memories were still vivid among Irish followers and whetted the appetite for more of the same stirring stuff.

The summer prelim was hardly all that conducive towards Irish confidence. The touring side was 'moidered' in Brisbane but did much better in Perth. And coach Warren Gatland was getting matters better organised as the World Cup loomed. The autumn win over Argentina at Lansdowne Road appeared to instil much-needed confidence in the squad.

Ireland's talismanic hooker Keith Wood drives for the line to score against the USA. Wood scored four tries in the match, a new record for a hooker in an international.

And so to the opening Pool E match, the meeting of Ireland and the USA at Lansdowne Road on the evening of Saturday 2 October, just 24 hours before the Australians commenced their proceedings against Romania at Ravenhill. The feature in Dublin was the four tries from the Irish hooker, Keith Wood, which had the US coach, Jack Clark, describing Wood as 'if not the best hooker in the world, then very close to it'.

Ireland's 53-8 win was half the England win (106-8) over the US four weeks previously, but this time the US team had sharpened up its game considerably. Their concentration in what Jack Clark described as 'a David and Goliath thing' was on big hits and tight defence. But the Irish scrum was much better, and the line outs were virtually a disaster area for the Americans. Only their captain and No. 8, Dan Lyle, measured up in skill and athleticism to the Irish forward opposition. Indeed it was strange that with so many tall players in the line out the Americans should lose so much of their own ball.

David Humphreys landed his first penalty goal after a mere three minutes and was to go on to land, successfully, all six of his goal kicks. Then, a few minutes later, right wing Justin Bishop turned up in the middle to cleave through for a try at the posts, which Humphreys converted to give Ireland a ten-nil lead. Minutes after that, the Irish fringe defence was caught unawares and Kevin Dalzell, the American scrum half, got over for his try. It was 10-5 for Ireland after ten minutes.

But it didn't herald any real USA challenge. The Americans certainly hit with powerful tackles, but the Irish were getting their machine into gear. Their pack, so well led by their skipper – No. 8 Dion O'Cuinneagain, who is South African-born of Irish parents – was just too strong and more technically adept. And the half backs, scrum half Tom Tierney and out-half Humphreys, were coolly controlling affairs. Brian O'Driscoll, not yet 21 and a most promising centre, showed his flair and speed for a try which Humphreys converted to increase the lead to 17-5. Dalzell got the USA's only other score with a penalty goal, but Keith Wood sent Ireland into the dressing room happy enough at half-time when he crashed over from a maul for his first try, which Humphreys duly converted to make it 24-8 at the interval. It was all

Ireland in the second half, beginning with a penalty try and Humphreys adding a penalty goal to that conversion. Then came the virtuoso display by hooker Wood with three more tries in the last ten minutes. Eric Elwood, who had replaced Humphreys, converted two of them.

The Australians made their first match appearance the day after the Irish had accounted for the USA. Having prepared in the salubrious surroundings of the Portmarnock Hotel and Golf Links on the seashore north of Dublin, they played Romania just a hundred miles further north at Belfast's Ravenhill ground. And the Australian margin of victory was much similar to that achieved by Ireland. The Wallabies scored nine tries and confined the Romanians to a mere three penalty goals, kicked by their very useful scrum half, Petre Mitu.

The Australian display was far from faultless. One newspaper headline summed up the situation: 'Ring-rusty Wallabies do enough'. They made a surprising number of handling errors – 23 – and even managed to lose three of their own line outs. But they were still far too good for Romania, and one shudders to think how much wider the 57-9 margin would have been had Australia been really in tune. The conventional wisdom was that the Wallabies were out of 'synch' because of the month's lay-off since their previous Test, but subsequent events against Ireland would clearly indicate that one match was insufficient to get the machine purring at maximum efficiency.

The Aussies were 24-3 up at half-time. There was one try from Tim Horan (who scored within two minutes of the kick-off and earned a £10,000 cheque from Guinness for the charity of his choice), two from No. 8 Toutai Kefu, and one from Jason Little just on half-time. Matt Burke converted two and Mitu replied for Romania with his first penalty goal. In the second half Australia scored five further tries – two from Joe Roff, a third from Kefu, and one each from hooker Jeremy Paul and full back Matt Burke, who converted his own and two others; John Eales converted the final try, which was Kefu's hat-trick score. The Romanians, clearly wilting in the final stages, contributed two second-half penalty goals by Mitu.

Not many spectators turned up on the eve of the 'Big One' in Pool E to watch the so-called 'minnows', the USA and Romania, in action at Lansdowne Road. A pity, because it turned out to be quite an entertaining joust. The US dominated the first half and appeared to be cruising to a win when they led 17-5 at half-time. The injured US captain, Dan Lyle, retired after half an hour, and the

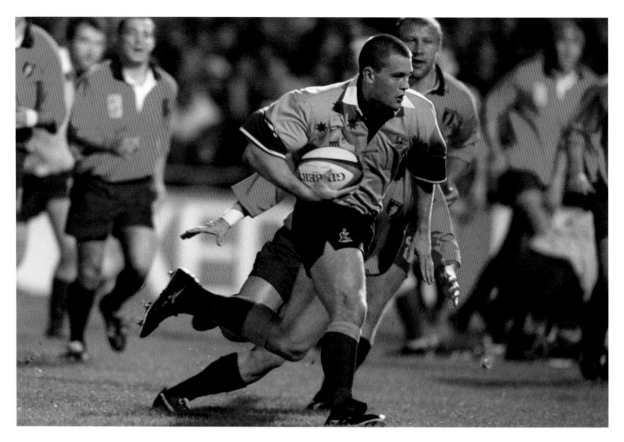

Ben Tune in full flight against Romania. Although he failed to make the scoresheet in this game, the big Australian wing is one of the most effective finishers in world rugby.

pendulum swung Romania's way in the second half. Much of the credit goes to their captain, Tudor Constantin, who had missed the Australian match but now returned to inspire his side to a 27-25 win, almost a 'Rising of Lazarus' affair. Kevin Dalzell, the US scrum half, failed with a late conversion that would have drawn the match.

And how did this result serve as a pointer to the next day's affair between Ireland and Australia? Form might suggest that as both Romania and the USA had previously been beaten by fairly similar scores the signs were that the Irish and the Aussies were fairly evenly matched. The pre-match atmosphere at Lansdowne Road on that Sunday afternoon of 10 October was tremendous. It was colourful, bright, noisy and cheerful. The Irish followers' rendering of 'The Fields of Athenry' was as spirited and as happy as ever it has been. The big concourse of Australian supporters was by no means outshouted or outsung. 'Waltzing Matilda' raised the rafters too. So, the overture was superb. Pity about the performance itself.

The game got a terrible press. 'It was awful, comfortably the poorest game of the tournament to date' was one account, and 'it was a miracle that the crowd even stayed to the end'. 'This was a quite terrible game, the worst I have seen in years' was another verdict, voicing the opinions of many. Was it that bad? And were there any decent excuses for the poor quality? The players on both teams did refer to the strong swirling wind. Australia's David Wilson told a press conference that 'it was a difficult match to play in. There was a big swirling wind. I mean you can't throw your cut-out passes, which is a way of getting around the opposition. Also balls in the air were very difficult to catch.'

From quite early it was clear that Australia were far the better side. They owned the rucks 74 to 36. In open play they won the ball 76 times to Ireland's 38. The great mystery was that with all that possession and the wind blowing in their favour they were only two penalty goals to nil ahead at half-time. That Ireland kept the damage down to a mere three points until injury time in the first half was quite incredible. That opening penalty goal had come from full back Matt Burke after nine minutes, but

Tudor Constantin, the Romania second-row and captain, stands tall in the line to take the ball during his side's 27-25 victory over the USA at Lansdowne Road.

after that he was to miss with two very makeable shots at goal, as did John Eales with one from farther out. Then, in the 43rd minute of proceedings, the Irish full back, Conor O'Shea, high-tackled Stephen Larkham, Eales found the range, and Ireland went to their dressing room at the interval feeling that, maybe, the Wallabies were 'catchable' in the second half.

So much for fond hopes. A circle of the Irish players sang spiritedly before the second half start, but any inspiration to improve was still very much absent. The Australians continued to own the ball on the ground. Players like No. 8 Toutai Kefu, Eales, David Wilson and company were yards faster, and apart from Keith Wood – sometimes – in the loose and in the set scrums, the Irish were simply outclassed. Ireland scrum half Tom Tierney

Below: Full back Kurt Shuman touches down in the corner in the 78th minute to take the US to within two points of Romania. Sadly for them, Kevin Dalzell could not convert.

Tom Tierney lines up a clearance kick under the watchful gaze of Wallaby flanker Mark Connors. The Irish scrum half had a tough afternoon – and so did his forwards.

had a difficult afternoon but was not helped much by an Irish back row that didn't appear to be in real communication with him. So, with hasty and sparse possession, out-half David Humphreys had little influence on affairs either. Nor did full back O'Shea, who was having one of those strange days in his relationship with the rolling ball. But the great disappointment for the Irish supporters was the total inability of the Irish pack to match the Australians in striving for possession. The Australians were physically stronger, and they made the Irish look lethargic in comparison. It was all so far distant from 1991. The 1999 Australians were not only superior in skill, physique and speed, they also were much more committed to their task.

Yet, why did it take them so long to put the game out of Ireland's reach? Rod Macqueen, Australia's coach, put it down to 'the difficulty of stringing passes together, and we often dropped the ball', and he echoed David Wilson's point about the swirling wind as a big problem. Certainly the Australians showed great respect for that wind. Time and again, despite all the time in the world to move the

ball wide, scrum half George Gregan and his outside partner, Stephen Larkham, preferred the option of moving back to their forwards for yet another bulldozing assault on the massed Irish. And it was not just good Irish defence that frustrated them until midway through the second half, when, at last, Tim Horan made the 'Great Breakthrough'. There were many handling errors, stray passes, forward passes; and, as in Belfast in their opening game against Romania, the ring-rustiness – or was it that wind? – exhibited itself again.

Just after the restart, Matt Burke made it 9-0 with a penalty goal, and shortly afterwards Humphreys got Ireland's only three points of the afternoon. Then, 17 minutes into the second half, Tim Horan, with one of the few pieces of creativity of the day, flashed through the Irish midfield, scored his try at the posts and Burke made it 16-3, sealing the issue. There was an even classier bit of Aussie skill near the end when Gregan's reverse pass sent Joe Roff away and Horan linked with Ben Tune on the right for a try in the corner. Burke – with total contempt for that Lansdowne breeze – converted from way out for a 23-3 win and a sigh of relief.

The Irish coach, Warren Gatland, summed up the Irish thoughts on affairs: 'A very disappointing performance,' he labelled it. 'We were well beaten by a very good Australian team and one of the most annoying things was that we didn't even fire a shot.' But if there were no shots, there were a few punches. There was, in the second half, the astonishing sight of a confrontation between the Irish flanker Trevor Brennan and the Aussie No. 8, Toutai Kefu. Whatever Brennan did, Kefu more than repaid with a rapid succession of rights and lefts. Touch judge Brian Campsall intervened, and when things quietened down, referee Clayton Thomas awarded a penalty kick to Australia, which caused some surprise. Both Brennan and Kefu – and managers – were summoned to London, and the decision of the RWC three-man disciplinary committee was a 14-day suspension for Kefu and a ten-day ban for Brennan. Another citing, for a

high tackle by Aussie centre Dan Herbert on his Irish counterpart Kevin Maggs, was, as expected, dismissed.

After that, with Australia left with just a visit to Limerick to take on the USA in their final pool match, Rod Macqueen went public to declare his dissatisfaction with too many so-called 'minnows' having been allowed into the final stages. Ironically, quicker than you could say Jack Robinson – or Rod Macqueen, if you prefer – the Samoans came up with the most practical of ripostes in Cardiff. Still, it was a second team that Australia chose for the engagement with the USA that followed their

Irish flanker Trevor Brennan is separated from Wallaby No. 8 Toutai Kefu after their second-half dust-up. Kefu was banned for 14 days; Brennan for ten.

Springbok-turned-Wallaby Tiaan Strauss is held by US centre Alatini Saulala in Australia's final Pool E match, in Limerick. Strauss scored a try in the Wallabies' 55-19 win.

success over Ireland. Only Stephen Larkham, Mark Connors and Matt Burke, who played at centre, joined the shadow Aussie XV for the match at Thomond Park, which the IRFU had recently upgraded at a cost of £3 million. Typically of Limerick – the 'spiritual home of Irish rugby' – a capacity crowd of 12,000 thronged the Park.

Meanwhile, the Irish, who had been slated by the critics ('Where's your pride, Ireland?'), decided to rest most of the side for their final pool match, against Romania at Lansdowne Road. The original selection had nine changes, and full back Conor O'Shea was named captain. But in the light of their previous outing, sarcasm and satire ruled the build-up among the supporters. 'How will the coach know which is the first team and which is the shadow team?' was one sardonic query.

The Australians scored eight tries in Limerick and won after a scintillating second half of marvellous angled running. But in the first half they found the wholehearted Americans playing their best football of the tournament. The USA scored a try just before half-time for the Australians to lead by an unimpressive 22-10 at the

interval. No doubt, Rod Macqueen had a word or two about minnows during the break. The US try was scored wide out on the left by centre Juan Grobler, and captain for the day Kevin Dalzell converted. Earlier, that gifted out-half David Niu had dropped a goal. The crowd were behind the underdogs and would have dearly loved to see the Australians discomfited by another US try. But it was not to be. The only further dividends to accrue to the USA were three penalty goals by Dalzell.

Australia scored three tries in the first half – one from Stephen Larkham, a second from very speedy wing Scott Staniforth, and a late one from a maul on the line by hooker Michael Foley. Matt Burke converted two and kicked a penalty goal, and the Australians retired at half-time needing a much-improved second half to salvage some pride and reputation. Which they certainly produced. It was a thorough transformation. The Australian second-half display was an object lesson for those who would aspire to creative rugby. There were the shrewd promptings of out-half Larkham and never a shortage of superb athletes eager to batten on everything he offered. And none was more eager or impressive than wing Scott Staniforth, who scored two dashing tries, the second just a minute into the second half from the neatest of chip kicks by Larkham. Then followed a score by Matt Burke, put clear by another pacy bit of work by Staniforth. Back-row forward Tiaan Strauss scored his try, and then the two Chrises – full back Latham and scrum half Whitaker – added a couple to round off affairs. Matt Burke converted four of the five – and Australia were duly on their way to Cardiff for the quarter-finals.

And would the Romanians put an end to Ireland's World Cup progress the following evening? As it happened, the answer was a resounding 'No' as an Irish side with a fair quota of second choices ensured their country's second, and qualifying, place behind Australia in Pool E with a clearcut 44-14 win. Those Irish supporters who had watched with dismay the performance against Australia could hardly believe the difference. Eric Elwood, who had been very much in the shadow of David Humphreys, gave a masterly display against the Romanians. His tactical kicking and his passing were superb and he was successful with all seven of his place-kicks. It was Elwood's best Test performance in three years agreed coach Warren Gatland. And who will play in

Lens in the play-offs, Humphreys or Elwood? 'Isn't it a very nice problem to have?' said the Irish coach.

The Romanians were well shackled from an early stage, and the Irish defence was impregnable. True, Romania scored a try through their wing Cristian Sauan, but that was in the closing stages when replacements were joining in hordes and there was general disruption. The point about the Irish defence that would have particularly pleased Gatland was that on their last visit to Ireland the previous November the Romanians had scored five tries. Dion O'Cuinneagain, the Irish captain, was drafted in not long before the kick-off due to injury problems, and his display of skill, speed and athleticism was outstanding. For Ireland there were five tries – two from O'Shea, one each from Andy Ward, Tom Tierney and O'Cuinneagain – and Elwood's 100 per cent place-kicking. Besides Sauan's try, the Romanian points were three penalties from Mitu.

Given the fly half berth against Romania, Eric Elwood took full advantage, kicking seven goals and making a firm bid for a place in the Irish team for the quarter-final play-offs.

Gets the lads buzzing.

J. LEWSEY.
*Celebrating winning the
Tetley's Bitter Cup.*

T18.

THE T18 COMES EQUIPPED WITH AN IN-BUILT
SILENT VIBRATING ALERT...

GREAT FOR DISCREET CELEBRATIONS.

Ericsson. Proud sponsors of London Wasps Rugby Football Club.

Make yourself heard.   www.ericsson.co.uk   **ERICSSON**

Quarter-Final Play-Off

England v Fiji

Alastair Hignell

England hooker Phil Greening struggles to get away from Fiji centre Meli Nakauta. Greening topped off a fine performance with England's fourth try in the 68th minute.

Yes, well, but... England won, by a convincing margin, and in the process scored some brilliantly executed tries. But their much-vaunted defence was shredded at times by Fiji's ebullient and inventive approach play, their midfield was exposed as the pedestrian combination many had feared it would be, and several key players were forced off by injury just four days before the quarter-final against the world champions. There was no doubt that England deserved to win. Their pack, led from the front by Martin Johnson and Lawrence Dallaglio, was superb, they seized their try-scoring opportunities with aplomb, and Jonny Wilkinson was punishingly accurate with the boot. The Newcastle prodigy, who left the field after being injured in setting up England's final try, landed three penalties in the first 15 minutes of each half, first to settle any early England nerves, then to kill off any Fijian hopes of a revival.

While England coach Clive Woodward had taken a calculated gamble in resting key players like prop Phil Vickery and second-row Danny Grewcock, and leaving others like Matt Dawson, Richard Hill and Phil de Glanville on the bench, Fiji's Brad Johnstone sprang a couple of late surprises by waiting until the morning of the match before announcing that Waisale Serevi would start at outside half instead of Nicky Little, and that Meli Nakauta would replace Waisake Sototu at centre.

Serevi was instantly successful with the boot, a fourth-minute penalty cancelling out Wilkinson's opening effort, and as playmaker he co-ordinated the series of sweeping attacks with which Fiji finished the half. As decision-maker, however, his preference for turning penalties into attacking line outs on England's line rather than taking close-range shots at goal with the wind behind him contributed greatly to England's weathering of the storm.

By half-time England had scored two well-worked tries of their own. A series of attacks down the right, in which Beal, Perry and Dallaglio were prominent, was nearly wasted when a huge ballooned pass from Healey bounced tantalisingly within reach of the Fijian midfield. A courageous dive from Wilkinson rescued the situation before quick hands allowed Neil Back to put left wing Dan Luger into space. A dazzling burst of pace took him outside cover tackles from flankers Sewabu and Tawake, while raw power enabled him to shrug off the challenge of full back Uluinayau and coast over under the posts for his eleventh try in 14 starts.

England's second try was also scored down the left, after Johnson and Dallaglio had made the vital yards down the right. This time, in a well-rehearsed move, Wilkinson kicked high to the corner, where Neil Back

Fiji scrum half Mosese Rauluni whips the ball out to replacement fly half Nicky Little. Their exuberant style brought Fiji three tries – and they might have had more.

timed his run, leap and catch to perfection. Back's try relieved the pressure for England after Fiji had enjoyed their best period of the match. A stunning counterattack led by Satala and Tikomaimakogai was halted only when Nick Beal dived over a ruck to prevent quick release of the ball, and received a yellow card for his pains. Then, after a quickly taken tapped penalty, former Leicester wing Marika Vunibaka was put through a gap only to drop the ball with the try line at his mercy. Next Tikomaimakogai dropped a scoring pass in midfield after Serevi had looped his centres, and Vunibaka, from the opposite wing, and Uluinayau had created the overlap.

A breathless finish to the half left England decidedly lucky to go into the break 21-3 ahead. Injuries to Luger, Healey and Worsley meant that Woodward had to use de Glanville, Dawson and Hill rather earlier than he had hoped. Their presence encouraged England to restore the shape to their game and create the positions from which Wilkinson kicked a couple of penalties. Before he could kick his third, however, Fiji's own substitution had borne fruit. Nicky Little had been on for only three minutes in place of Serevi when he found a gap on England's left and sent centre Vili Satala in for a try which Little converted.

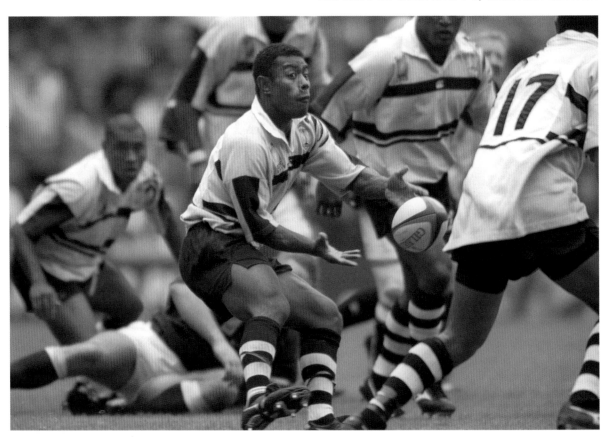

Imanueli Tikomaimakogai clings on to his opposite number, Dan Luger. Luger got his name on the scoresheet in the 23rd minute; Tikomaimakogai added his in the second half.

Little also converted Fiji's second try, scored by Tikomaimakogai after England had failed to read any danger in a kick ahead that, to be fair, seemed more hopeful than calculated, but by that time England had scored another beauty of their own. Again Dallaglio made the initial inroad, this time down the left wing from the back of a set scrum. Dawson's tapped penalty had the Fijians back-pedalling furiously, and two long passes, the last from Matt Perry, gave Beal a clear run at the right-hand corner. Wilkinson's seventh penalty from eight attempts was followed by England's fourth try. Sale hooker Phil Greening, conspicuous throughout, rounded off another multiphased attack from England, but Wilkinson was hurt in the act of delivering the pass, leaving Dawson to take the conversion.

Of even more concern to Clive Woodward was the sight of Matt Perry leaving the field injured with two

Jonny Wilkinson was successful with seven penalties out of eight before being substituted after a blow to the head in setting up Phil Greening's try.

minutes to go. Perry had played more games for Woodward than any other player – appearing in 24 of the 28 teams Woodward had selected – but he damaged his shoulder stemming one late Fiji assault and aggravated it still further in a try-saving tackle on Setareki Tawake after Sewabu's chip and chase. England by this point had used all seven substitutes; their reintroduction of Worsley, 38 minutes after he had left the field for what was described as a 'blood injury', was controversial to say the least. With Worsley at No. 8 and Dallaglio treading unfamiliar ground at full back, England conceded a last-minute try to Meli Nakauta, which Little converted.

As the final whistle blew to leave England victors 45-24, Fiji's players received a standing ovation from a less than full Twickenham. The lap of honour they enjoyed was thoroughly deserved. They had contributed richly both to this match and to the whole tournament. They had made their mark on England quite literally and, with Smith's assault on Wilkinson going unpunished by the referee, quite legally. Their inventiveness, their lines of running and their close-quarter handling skills had given England's battered and bruised players plenty to think about as they made their way to Paris and a quarter-final with South Africa. The world champions wouldn't be losing any sleep over the impending showdown. England had paid a heavy price to reach this stage of the tournament. So far, it had all been worthwhile.

Very front row.

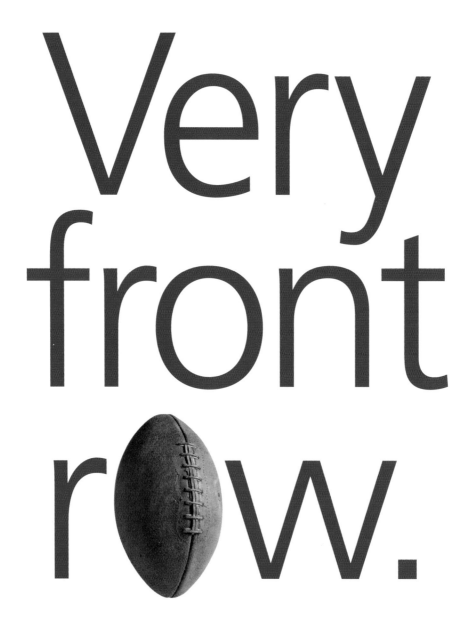

Strong Performance. **Solid** Delivery. **Disciplined** Investment Process.

Individual Savings Accounts (ISAs), PEP transfers, Pensions and Savings Plans, Investment Trusts and Open Ended Funds, Private Client Portfolio Management, Institutional Fund Management.

One of the largest independent fund management groups in the UK with £7.4 billion of funds under management.

Edinburgh
FUND MANAGERS

Regulated by IMRO and the Personal Investment Authority.

www.edfd.com   **0800 028 6789**

Quarter-Final Play-Off

Scotland v Samoa

Alan Lorimer

Referee David McHugh awards a penalty try to Scotland, believing that an infringement by the Samoa pack had stopped the Scots from scoring.

Was it to be a re-run of eight years ago when Scotland and Samoa met at Murrayfield in the quarter-final of RWC 1991, when, in an uncannily similar scenario to now, Samoa had come to Edinburgh fresh from a victory over Wales? Or could Samoa this time expunge the disappointing memory of their 1991 defeat by Scotland? Unlike in 1991 this was not a quarter-final but a play-off for a place in the last eight, a stage introduced because of the decision to have five pools of four in the group phase. For the victor there was a quarter-final against New Zealand, but both sides knew the likely cost in physical terms of having to play an extra match. Bryan Williams, for whom the Murrayfield play-off was his last game as coach of Samoa, articulated the thoughts of many on this subject when he said: 'The teams in the play-offs are really up against it. Having to play three Tests in eight or nine days is near impossible.'

Scotland had reached the play-offs by finishing second in the highly unbalanced Pool A that contained defending champions South Africa and the new entrants Spain and Uruguay. Scotland, other than in their opening match against the Springboks, had not been tested. Moreover, they had shared with South Africa the experience of playing against totally negative sides and performing only moderately against the tournament 'minnows'. The make-up of Pool A had also been a big turn-off for the Scottish public, who were further discouraged from attending World Cup games by the insensitively pitched prices and a schedule of matches that cut across normal work hours. Even so, it was intensely disappointing that only 15,500 spectators turned up at Murrayfield. The thousands who stayed away missed a game in which both Scotland and Samoa produced an impressive display of attacking football, creating the thrust and counterthrust that is the essence of spectacular rugby.

Jim Telfer and his coaching team had clearly noted the folly of Wales in attacking with a flat alignment and providing the hard-hitting Samoans with tasty midfield targets. Accordingly they had devised a strategy to minimise the risk of a repeat dosage. In the event Scotland attacked close to the fringe of the scrum and used a 'pick and drive' game that broke up the Samoans' defensive patterns. Moreover, Gregor Townsend, noted more as a running stand-off, showed another side to his game by using the long kick from hand to make territorial gains and to turn the Samoan defence.

Samoa, by contrast, looked at their elegant best when they spun the ball wide to give wingers Brian Lima and

Samoa full back Silao Leaega, supported by 'Inga the Winger', tries to give Scotland centre Jamie Mayer the slip at a sparsely populated Murrayfield.

Va'aiga Tuigamala and centre To'o Vaega chances to demonstrate running skills honed in sevens rugby or, in the case of the mighty 'Inga the Winger', in Rugby League. The problem, however, for the Samoans was in being able to secure quality set-piece ball, such was the pressure under which their scrum was forced to operate. Coach Bryan Williams revealed that they had lost two tight-head props just prior to the tournament and another at the pool stage. No team can afford these losses.

The Samoans' difficulties became evident right from the start when after an incredible series of ten scrums the Pacific islanders were deemed by referee David McHugh to have prevented a Scotland score. Another penalty try to add to the two conceded against Wales. 'A harsh decision,' suggested Samoa's inspirational captain, Pat Lam, playing his last match before retiring from international rugby. The fact that penalty tries are awarded under the posts and not at the place where the try would have been scored has always seemed slightly unfair. It certainly did to the Samoans, who watched Kenny Logan's conversion make it a seven-point offence.

Gregor Townsend heads for a gap inside Leaega, as Samoa skipper Pat Lam, who announced his retirement from international rugby after the match, closes in.

Scotland, too, attracted the attention of referee David McHugh, who was officiating instead of New Zealander Colin Hawke because it had been feared that as a New Zealander Hawke might influence the outcome of the game and hence which side the All Blacks would face in the quarter-finals. 'To suggest that a referee might have an influence when his country is not playing seems bizarre,' commented a baffled Bryan Williams. There was certainly no sense of bias when McHugh penalised Scotland after a tackle, allowing Samoa full back Silao Leaega to kick a simple goal. Scotland soon reasserted themselves, though, with a series of forward drives and some close inter-passing by the backs which ended with flanker Martin Leslie going over for an unconverted try.

The first half ended with Logan and Leaega each kicking a further goal, leaving Scotland ahead by 15-6 at the interval. It was a lead which the Scots were to stretch as their pressure in the third quarter yielded three penalty goals by Logan to bump the score up to 24-6. Then, when Townsend finished a superb move by the Scots with a dropped goal it seemed all over for the Samoans with the scoreline reading 27-6. The Pacific islanders, however, were far from finished and showed as much by moving the ball wide to involve the powerful Tuigamala and the quicksilver Vaega before flanker Semo Sititi touched down for a typical Samoa try. Leaega added the

conversion, and Samoa were back in the game. But then a Logan penalty and a try by Cameron Murray from a counterattack by Townsend ensured the Scots of victory, despite a stylish finish by the Samoans that ended with their veteran wing Brian Lima racing in for his side's second try. Leaega added the easy conversion to make Samoa's final tally 20 to Scotland's 35.

It was a fitting way for Samoa to bow out of the tournament. Their style of rugby had been effective and entertaining and in many ways not dissimilar to Scotland's. As in 1991, the Samoans were given generous applause for their efforts, but once again their guns had not been big enough where it mattered. For Scotland, captained by Gary Armstrong in his 50th international, there was the satisfaction of defeating Samoa when it mattered after an indifferent display in the drawn match four years previously at Murrayfield. It was a performance that compared with the 1991 victory, but for those who recall the then Scotland back row of Calder, White and Jeffrey, there must have been a sense of dismay when Cameron Mather came on as a replacement to make the present back row temporarily an all Kiwi affair. Where have all the Scotland flankers gone?

The opportunity: Europe.
The investment: Newton.

- Privatisation; economic recovery; attractive valuations. Continental Europe remains a key investment theme for 1999.

- The Newton Universal Growth Fund Continental European Equity Fund has an award-winning performance record. Return over 1, 3 and 5 years up to 1st October 1999 on an Offer to Bid basis is as follows:**

Newton Universal Growth Fund Continental European Equity Fund	
One Year	8.62%
Three Years	89.19%
Five Years	177.85%

"We believe that Europe offers some of the world's most promising opportunities for enhanced returns through 1999 and that the Newton Continental European Fund continues to be well placed to outperform against this background."

Keiran Gallagher, Fund Manager

For more information contact Rachael Glover-Wright in Jersey:

Tel   (+44)   1534   285707
Fax   (+44)   1534   285751

or Connie Fung in Hong Kong on:

Tel   (+852)   2824   8423
Fax   (+852)   2824   8076

NEWTON

Quarter-Final Play-Off

Ireland v Argentina

Mick Cleary

For the first time in four World Cups, Argentina reached the knockout stage, facing Ireland at Lens for a place in the quarter-finals. That in itself, considering their recent chequered history, was a considerable advance and – they freely admitted – a cause for celebration. And for Ireland, who had always reached the quarter-final stage in the previous World Cups, and considering Argentina's improving form, it was a cause for a fair degree of nervousness. Ireland's coach, Warren Gatland, had admitted beforehand that he would have preferred to have the Samoans in opposition rather than the Argentinians. His reading of the situation was that Ireland would be confident of handling the Samoans in the set pieces. But taking on the strong Argentinian pack, he felt, was a different and more onerous job.

For a country which is very much removed from being among the so-called 'minnows' of the game, Argentina's World Cup record has been awful. Until RWC 1999 they had lost eight of their nine ties. Their only success was a win over Italy in 1987; they lost their other two matches in that tournament. They lost all three in 1991 and 1995. And all the signs were that internal dissension would once again ensure little improvement. But, ironically, the resignation of two coaches on the eve of the tournament paved the way for their New Zealand technical advisor, the highly experienced Alex Wyllie, to take over as coach. And it seemed that the upgrading of Wyllie might have done the trick. Just five points separated Argentina from Wales (18-23) in the opening game of the tournament in Cardiff on the first day of October, and they won their next two matches without too much trouble. They beat the uninhibited Samoans 32-16 in Llanelli and then carefully saw off the Japanese 33-12 in Cardiff to qualify, as the best third-placed team, for the tilt in Lens.

There was still an element of the unknown about the Irish as they arrived in Lens. They beat the USA comfortably enough (53-8) in Dublin without exactly setting the bonfires blazing. But in the much heralded re-run of the famous 1991 Ireland v Australia clash, the Wallabies hardly needed to get out of second gear to win 23-3. And the Irish supporters, expecting so much more, were highly critical of an Ireland performance that lacked

Ireland centre Brian O'Driscoll arrives just too late to stop Argentinian left wing Diego Albanese crossing for the only try of the game in the 73rd minute.

the usual spirit. The dismissal of Romania 44-14 to qualify for Lens was a vast improvement but had been produced by a mainly second team. So Lens was make or break for Irish rugby.

As it transpired, it was break — with a vengeance. Ireland led 21-9 just after half-time. David Humphreys was ahead in his personal place-kicking duel with Gonzalo Quesada, but the crucial moment arrived in the 73rd minute when Argentina scored the only try of the game. It was the little left wing, Diego Albanese, who romped over, and the conversion by Quesada, who had earlier kicked a couple more penalties, put Argentina ahead 24-23. Everything else after that was a mere crossing of 't's' and dotting of 'i's'. Argentina were en route for Lansdowne Road and the quarter-final with France in the biggest day in their rugby history.

The battle of Lens was a bizarre affair, with the Australian referee, Stuart Dickinson, ensuring it would be so: he awarded 33 penalties — 17-16 in favour of the Pumas — with a pedantic application of the laws and a total lack of sympathy for the ebb and flow of the game. He had virtually a fetish about players staying on their

Irish hooker Keith Wood runs at the Argentinian defence. Try as they might, Ireland could find no way through the Pumas' lines at Lens.

feet — with the Irish the chief offenders — but a more liberal use of the advantage law would surely have led to a more entertaining evening. As it was, the local French spectators in the half-filled stadium were less than enchanted with the fare and made their feelings clear with some solid rounds of booing. And any support they gave was to the Argentinians, who tried, at least, to open up the game a bit in contrast to the dull Irish, whose tactics were confined to ineffective forward bullocking.

It was 15-9 for Ireland at half-time. They had the majority of possession, and Humphreys had slotted over five penalty goals, including one from halfway. Quesada had scored three for Argentina in reply. Overall, if anything can be praised about this Lens affair it is the superb place-kicking of this pair. In the second half Humphreys kicked two more penalties and dropped a goal, but he did miss with two further dropped goal attempts, hitting an upright with one of them. Indeed, it was the Argentinian adrenalin which flowed more purposefully in the second half, with scrum half Agustin Pichot prompting cleverly and centre Lisandro Arbizu chip-kicking neatly and passing intelligently. Ireland, in contrast, confined their endeavours to trying to barge their way through a very effective Puma defensive curtain. Not once did they look like succeeding, and their efforts become more and more frustrated.

Elation and euphoria for Argentina as Stuart Dickinson blows the final whistle at Lens. For the first time in four World Cups, the Pumas had made it to the knockout stage.

Ireland had every chance to come back after Quesada had added another penalty to put Argentina 28-24 ahead, because Mr Dickinson found it necessary to play eight minutes of injury time. Ireland massed desperately on the Argentinian line in those closing minutes and used the noted Warren Gatland ploy of putting the entire team into a line out. Yet despite a succession of penalties – and a feeling that a penalty try should have accrued – the Argentinian defence was equal to Ireland's fierce assaults.

So despite David Humphreys' dropped goal and seven penalties for all Ireland's 24 points, it was Quesada with his 23 points – seven penalties and a conversion – and Argentina who triumphed 28-24 because of that tricky bit of running and that try by Albanese. A great day for the Pumas, but one of the blackest days in Irish rugby history. Afterwards Warren Gatland was quoted as saying when asked 'Whither Ireland now?': 'We'll just have to sit back, regroup and look forward to the Six Nations Championship.' Which brought from one Irish commentator the riposte: 'That is the equivalent of a failed Olympic sprinter pronouncing enthusiastically on the forthcoming parish egg-and-spoon race.'

Meanwhile, spare a thought for the Irish. It is all too obvious how much the World Cup meant to Paul Wallace, Eric Miller and Kieron Dawson.

NEXT

Official Clothing Sponsors
Leicester Tigers

Quarter-Final
Wales v Australia
Eddie Butler

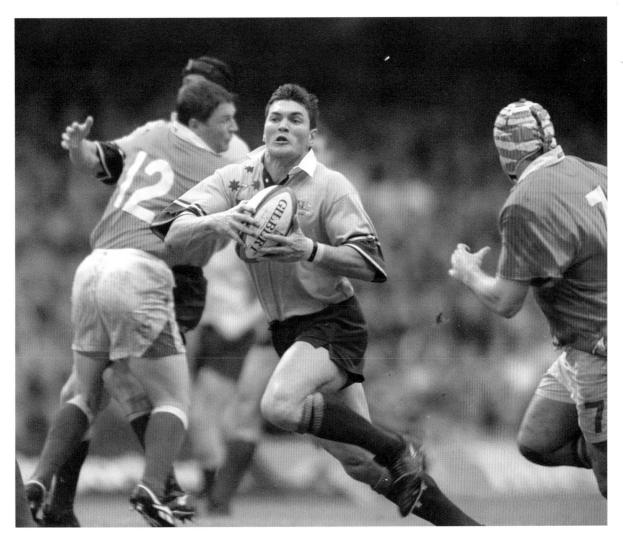

Wallaby centre Daniel Herbert sniffs a gap in the Welsh midfield and takes off. At 6ft 2ins and almost 16 stones, and with plenty of pace, he takes some stopping!

Even defeat against Samoa had failed to quash the suspicion that the World Cup draw had been neatly fiddled to suit Wales. The host nation in the two previous tournaments had shared the same group as the defending champions, but expansion from 16 to 20 teams, and from four groups to five, had given Wales unexpected protection from South Africa; in fact, from all the Tri-Nations teams. But now it became clear that the fiddle could also play a heavy tune. Three group winners – New Zealand, South Africa and France – would play the victors of the midweek scramble, the supplementary play-off round. But two group winners would have to play each other – D against E: Wales against Australia.

Some fiddle! Australia had beaten the All Blacks in the final Test of the Tri-Nations and had then slipped down a few gears to ease without strain past Ireland, Romania and the USA. When asked if he could think of any weaknesses in the Wallaby team, Welsh coach Graham Henry said, 'None.' He went further: 'Australia

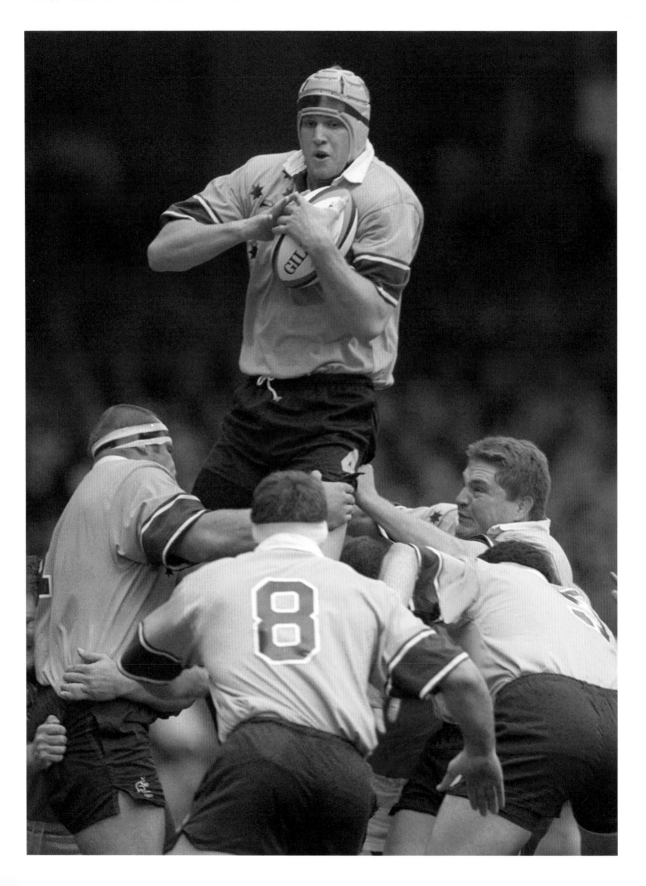

are the best sporting nation in the world. If we don't play way above what we've managed so far, we're going to be humiliated.' Australia had beaten Wales in their previous six meetings, and most of those victories had contained no small element of embarrassment. And yet, the feeling could not yet be completely quelled that Wales still had a chance. 'He's just playing mind games, our Graham,' was the consensus in Cardiff. 'You never know.'

Perhaps he knew only too well. Wales played by far the best rugby of their World Cup, and it wasn't enough. They had a measure of bad luck in that the try at the end of the game, which gave the score a lop-sided look, should never have been awarded, but the issue had been settled by then. Australia were too strong and too smart.

The game divided neatly into four strategic quarters which more or less aped the 20-minute divisions of the clock. In the opening period Wales were as nervous as they had been in their group games. Perhaps the atmosphere of home was simply too overwhelming, although the pockets of empty seats here and there all around the Millennium Stadium said more about ongoing ticketing problems than crushing Wales with love.

A poor start was the last thing Wales needed. If the Wallabies had a weakness, it was said that they themselves were sluggish at the outset. But they nearly scored after four minutes, and did cross the line after five. Wales were finding it more than just difficult to recycle the ball quickly after the tackle; they were already being turned over, victims of the opposing back row. Matt Cockbain was a thorn at the line out, Tiaan Strauss was massive in the tackle and David Wilson was a feisty old fox when it came to pinching ball Wales took into the ruck. Wales tried to develop a handling movement on their own 22, but the ruck they set up turned into a launch pad for Australia. Out came the ball on the Wallabies' side and away went Joe Roff down the blind side, his pass inside to George Gregan allowing the scrum half to slide over. Matt Burke converted from near the touch line.

If a warning bell had been sounded it was muffled just a couple of minutes later when Neil Jenkins was allowed a penalty shot at goal. There is no more reassuring sight in the Welsh game than the world record points scorer going through his routine, even if aiming from the touch line. Having not been in prime form in the group games,

'My ball, I think.' A soaring David Giffin, John Eales' partner in the Wallaby second row, collects at a line out, as No. 8 Tiaan Strauss moves in to help out.

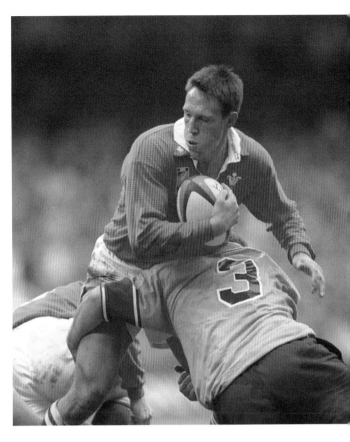

Mark Taylor's progress is arrested by Australia's Andrew Blades. Taylor and fellow Wales centre Scott Gibbs generally struggled to breach the Wallaby defensive wall.

he would return to immaculate form with his place-kicking here: over went his first penalty.

But the pattern remained the same in general play. Australia were more thrustful with their running, more powerful in the tackle. As the rain began to fall as a misty curtain, Wales persisted with their flat game, but whether he was passing outside to Scott Gibbs and Mark Taylor or inside to Scott Quinnell or Peter Rogers, Jenkins failed to launch any breaks through the defence. The turnovers continued, and Burke stretched his side's lead with a penalty. Australia had controlled the opening exchanges.

But then came the first shift. Wales tried a midfield move which saw Dafydd James and Mark Taylor cutting straight through. It led only to a penalty – against Scott Gibbs for obstruction – but if it seems ridiculous to applaud Wales for an illicit ploy that came to nothing, it was nonetheless the start of a more fluent period of play. Wales suddenly ran from a little deeper and made half a yard further through the tackle. The ball emerged cleanly from the rucks. Or if it did not it was because Australian hands were in the way, for which Jenkins made them pay with two penalties. The second of these was conceded by David Wilson for a piece of cheek whereby he simply stood offside and picked the ball up in the middle of a ruck. He had a wonderful game, as usual, but he should at least have been yellow-carded for this infringement.

Labelled 'Nobody', because 'Nobody's perfect', Australian captain John Eales lays the ball off to his waiting backs. Eales still seemed less than 100 per cent fit in this game.

Following pages: Scrum half George Gregan skips for joy as referee Colin Hawke awards Australia their third try, while the Wales players claim the ball had earlier gone forward.

He should also have been awarded a try later in the game. He was one of the players to show up the indifferent performance of Colin Hawke, the referee, who, even before all this, had penalised the scrummage by numbers. Throughout the first half he seemed to blow for and not against the side who was turning the scrummage inwards. Front-row play is one of the most esoteric pleasures in sport. The World Cup is no place to mount a campaign to try to master its many contortions.

Basically, referees understand the scrum as little as the 12 players on each side who would do anything rather than go up into the madhouse. And yet, it seemed that the scrummage had been pinpointed for a purge by the powers that be, and if a referee wanted a semi-final or the final, then he'd better prove he pretended to know what was going on among the last of the true specialists of the game. David Young had obviously had enough. The prop who first appeared as a teenager in the World Cup of 1987 limped off on a damaged calf – a proxy physical injury for the mental anguish of it all – at the end of the first half. The Welsh scrummage was never really comfortable after his exit.

Despite this discomfort the third quarter was a stalemate. At least as far as point-scoring was concerned. Nil-all for 20 minutes of the second half. But Australia were cranking up the power. Wales spent long periods deep in their own 22. Brett Sinkinson, outstanding throughout the World Cup, made a try-saving tackle underneath the posts; Shane Howarth – another Welsh-Kiwi and star of the tournament – leapt to claim a catch when the line was exposed.

Wales rarely threatened at the other end. Neil Jenkins tried to drop a goal but did not hit it sweetly. Allan Bateman replaced Gareth Thomas and added some grace to the counterattack; but who was going to provide the spark that would settle everything? He was more likely to be Australian than Welsh. Although only one point separated the sides – 10-9 to the Wallabies – the green-gold momentum seemed irresistible. Would it be John Eales' moment to announce his return to world-class

Opposite page: Second five-eighth (or inside centre) Tim Horan tries in vain to evade the grasp of flanker Brett Sinkinson, one of the stars of Wales' World Cup campaign.

Above: Another of Wales' World Cup stars was full back Shane Howarth, here held fast by George Gregan and David Giffin as Scott Gibbs and Craig Quinnell look on.

form? No, he was still not timing it right at the line out; his groin strain was still troubling him. Matt Burke perhaps; another on his way back from injury? No, he was not yet back to imperious form.

It was left to the five-eighths — Stephen Larkham, another who had long been absent through injury, and Tim Horan, still simply top-drawer — the one with the boot, the other by hand. It took a long time, but Larkham was the first to exploit the conditions. First he drilled Wales way back with a mark and punt. Then he threaded a kick behind the defence. The ball aquaplaned across the turf, pursued by Ben Tune for the converted try that left Wales needing two scores to win.

Left: Getting back in the groove after injury. Australia's first five-eighth (or fly half) and playmaker Stephen Larkham, whose kick ahead produced Ben Tune's try.

Right: The pain and strain of defeat shows on the face of hooker Garin Jenkins at full time as he contemplates the end of Wales' World Cup.

Only one came. And it fell to the Wallabies. Horan made a break, slipping out of tackles as if the rain had made him as uncatchable as the ball. Eventually he was tackled, and the ball spilled forward. All the Welsh bar Dafydd James stopped. Daniel Herbert and George Gregan kept going, the centre intelligently jostling James out of the way, allowing Gregan to claim his second try. Burke converted for a final score of 24-9 to Australia.

It summed up Colin Hawke's day. It sealed the game. It sent the crowd into a howling rage. But it did not affect the result. It merely confirmed that four years of anarchy in the rugby politics of Britain could not be repaired by a single year of Graham Henry; that the gulf between the hemispheres is still there; that the World Cup draw for Wales had been anything but a fiddle.

Below: Meanwhile its celebration time for Australian fans as they watch their team secure the first semi-final spot. But who would they play, England or the world champions?

You may never go there, but it's nice to know your phone will work if you do.

BT Cellnet. With roaming agreements in 100 different countries, no one else is as well connected.

iRB

RUGBY WORLD CUP 1999

Official mobile communications supplier Rugby World Cup 1999

BTcellnet
Good call

Beyond their wildest dreams! Springbok skipper Joost van der Westhuizen and Jannie de Beer can hardly contain themselves as the fly half's fifth dropped goal sails over.

H e doesn't look like a hit man. Fair complexion, tufty ginger hair, fresh smile and affable air, Jannie de Beer could easily pass for a head chorister at the local church. Indeed, given his devout Christian background, he most probably is. Yet, he took aim with the cold-eyed precision of an assassin on this mild, autumnal Paris afternoon, and struck England right between the eyes. Twelve times the trigger was cocked,

and 12 times de Beer hit the bullseye. The 28-year-old Springbok fly half finished with 34 points in all, a South African record. He had five dropped goals in that haul, beating the three-goal record previously achieved on eight occasions down the years.

De Beer was undoubtedly the headline star of the day. His goals drew the life from England. You could see the shock in their eyes as the right boot of the stand-off from Welkom in the Free State swung and made contact. Not once but five times the ball left his boot between the 43rd and 74th minutes. Each time, referee Jim Fleming sprinted towards the posts to follow the flight of the ball. And on each occasion the arm was raised to signal a goal.

De Beer was not even first choice for the match. The Boks had tried all manner of treatment to try and get Henry Honiball on the field. In the early season de Beer was even further down the rankings, perhaps as low as fifth choice. He had spent a season with London Scottish and had agreed terms with Sale for this season. The South Africans won't be letting go of him now.

How was it that England could get nowhere near him? Careful planning and precise execution is the answer. Springbok coach Nick Mallett read England perfectly. He knew it would be a tight game in theory so he planned accordingly. On a quiet, tree-fringed pitch at Boulogne-Bilancourt to the west of Paris, the Springboks went about their business, unnoticed and untroubled. England were not taking a blind bit of notice for the simple reason that they were still at home wrestling with the problem of how to deal with Fiji in a quarter-final play-off.

South Africa knew that they would be unlikely to score dropped goals from first phase. Neil Back and his mates in the England back row would see to that. Enter Pieter Muller into the equation. The 30-year-old from Bloemfontein, the only man in the squad to survive from South Africa's first post-isolation tour in 1992, was to be the donkey. A high-speed donkey it has to be said, who would do all the dirty work in order to set up position for de Beer. Muller would cut in from midfield, draw in the tackles from Back and the boys, recycle quickly, and there you have it. Simple and effective.

The still photographs from Monday's newspapers were revealing. They appeared identical, with de Beer's right leg swinging through and the ball passing the outstretched hands of an England player. Yet the England player in view varied from shot to shot. In one paper it was Jason Leonard; in another Danny Grewcock — a prop and a lock. The fast men were nowhere to be seen. The Springboks had done their homework and passed with flying colours.

Pieter Muller, a veteran of South Africa's 1992 tour, makes the hard yards and takes the hits from Phil de Glanville, Matt Dawson and Jonny Wilkinson.

Above: A face in the stands. England coach Clive Woodward cuts a rather forlorn figure as his side is closed down by a relentless South Africa at the Stade de France.

'I predicted that Jannie might get three of the drop goals,' said Mallett. 'But five is something special. We spent many hours on the video to study the way England played. We knew what they would serve up today.'

England had little idea what de Beer might serve up. Mind you, he had a guiding hand. 'There was something quite supernatural going on out there,' said de Beer. 'God gave us this victory. I am just happy to be part of His game plan. Things happen from time to time that you don't have an answer for. I personally feel that God had a hand in this. I thank the Lord for the talent He gave me and I thank the forwards for the ball they gave me.'

De Beer was right to salute his pack. They gave him all a fly half could have wished for. They were solid on their own ball and squeezed England on theirs. The English scrum was on the back foot for most of the game,

South Africa coach Nick Mallett has everything to smile about. His game plan has come together and his side is on the way to a semi-final against Australia at Twickenham.

The England pack holds firm, with Jason Leonard, Martin Johnson and Danny Grewcock to the fore. Overall, though, it was a tough day at the office for the England forwards.

not by much but by enough. It meant that the English back row were on their heels, not on their toes, and unable to launch themselves forwards; so too the half backs, Matt Dawson and a mix of Paul Grayson and Jonny Wilkinson.

Grayson had been brought in to put pressure on the Springbok rear three by pinning them back in the corners with long, raking kicks. The kicking game did not come

off, which is why Grayson did after 55 minutes play to be replaced by Wilkinson. Grayson had done wonderfully well with his goal-kicking up to that point. He converted four out of five attempts in the first half, two of them from

Above: Springbok full back Percy Montgomery and centre Robbie Fleck go ball-hunting as scrum half Joost van der Westhuizen waits and flanker Rassie Erasmus stands off.

England's Paul Grayson was in exceptional goal-kicking form, even banging them over from inside his own half. Here he strokes over one of his six penalty successes.

within his own half. Two more had gone over by the time he was substituted.

However, there was not enough variety in the England game. They stuck far too rigidly to a game plan that was obviously having little impact on their opponents. Once Wilkinson came on, there was a touch more dash and movement about the England back line. Even so they could make little headway against a cloying Springbok defence which swarmed all over England. There were often three or four tacklers converging on the one man.

What impact did the respective build-ups have? South Africa had only had one testing pool match in three weeks; England had had a testing play-off match only four days earlier. England captain Martin Johnson denied that it had made a difference. 'We didn't lose the game because we were tired,' said Johnson. 'It wasn't a factor.'

It didn't look that way from the stands. It was not that England trudged around the field, more that they couldn't really step up a gear when it counted. They didn't go about their business with the same ferocious zeal. More significantly, they were out-thought. Lawrence Dallaglio, such a prominent, influential figure throughout England's campaign, simply could not break free here. South Africa made sure that they kept the ball well away from him at restarts. Dallaglio spent too much time in the wide channels, looking to exploit space there. But the ball rarely came his way, South Africa cutting down England's midfield link of Phil de Glanville and Will Greenwood with brutal ferocity. 'They competed for everything on the

floor,' said Johnson. 'Their defence was outstanding. It was what made the difference on the day.' Mallett was generous enough to concede that the final scoreline did not quite reflect the run of play. 'The scoreboard flattered us,' said Mallett. 'It showed maybe ten points too many.'

It certainly did well to register the try scored by Joost van der Westhuizen four minutes before half-time. A skewed clearance from Grayson wobbled out towards the South African left wing. Nick Beal lost the ball in flight, enabling Pieter Rossouw to gather and set off into the England 22. He was tackled by de Glanville but managed

Oof! England's Matt Perry is hammered by Springbok No. 8 Bobby Skinstad. England skipper Martin Johnson later paid tribute to South Africa's 'outstanding' defence.

When you're on a roll... Jannie de Beer bisects the uprights and there is nothing England forwards Neil Back and Danny Grewcock can do about it.

to lay the ball back for Percy Montgomery, who picked up beautifully and steamed forward. The South African full back fed Muller in support, who, in turn, passed on to his captain. Van der Westhuizen was hit hard near the try line by Greenwood and Richard Hill. The South African scrum half managed to plant the ball down with one hand over the try line but appeared to make contact with his other arm on the corner flag. The try was given, however, and it was a real body blow to England.

De Beer converted from the touch line. Earlier he had kicked three penalties to give South Africa a 16-12 half-time lead. There was a sense then that England had to try something different. There seemed to be no chink in the South African armour that they could exploit by merely booming the ball downfield. Montgomery had invariably fielded the long kicks and returned them with interest. At times it was no better than aerial ping-pong as the ball sailed back and forth.

Grayson and de Beer continued their battle of the boot after the interval. Grayson struck two penalty goals, while the Springbok fly half knocked over his first two dropped goals. England gave away position for both those goals. Matt Perry tried to run from deep in the 43rd minute but was collared by Montgomery, then, two minutes later, Perry and de Glanville were flattened in midfield.

And so the pattern was set. Dawson tried to inject some spark into the English game with characteristic breaks, but he too was well shepherded. England could not shake off South Africa. Wilkinson missed his first shot at goal shortly after coming on in the 55th minute, but he made no mistake in the 62nd minute to close the gap to four points at 25-21. That was the end of England's scoring. The tide was green and gold from there on in. De Beer, whose third dropped goal went over in the 54th minute, struck two more in the 71st and 74th minutes. Two further penalty goals followed in quick succession.

De Beer was also involved in the last act of the day, hoisting a kick high to the wing. Dallaglio had his eye on André Venter, the ball bounced loose for Pieter Rossouw to gather and dive over. De Beer converted: 44-21 to South Africa. At the final whistle the South Africans dropped to their knees in a huddle to say a prayer. England merely dropped to their knees.

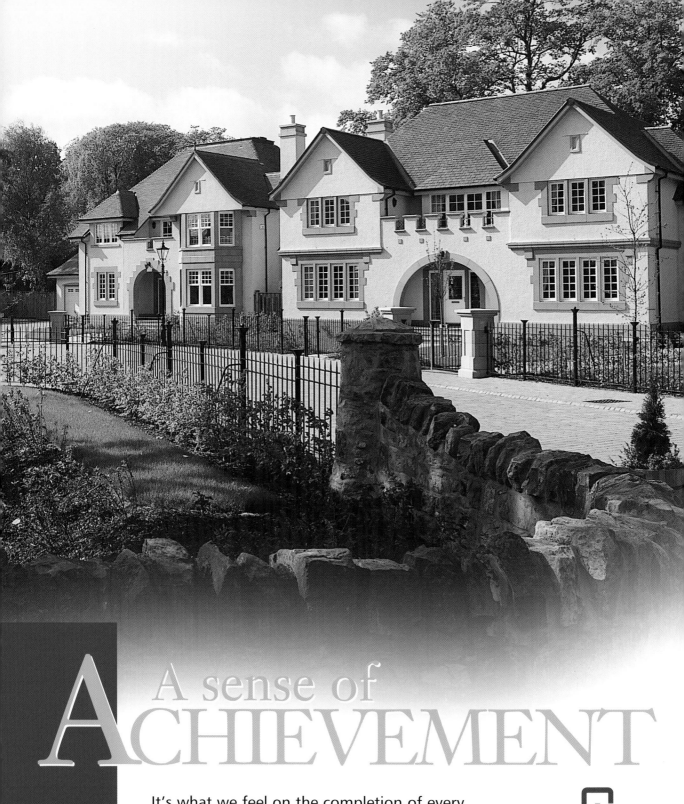

A sense of ACHIEVEMENT

It's what we feel on the completion of every CALA home.

It's what you feel when you live in one.

For further details of CALA developments please telephone: 01324 638889
www.pwave.co.uk/pwave/cala

Developments throughout Scotland

Quarter-Final
France v Argentina
Sean Diffley

Puma scrum half Agustin Pichot and wing Diego Albanese make themselves a Marc Lièvremont sandwich during the France v Argentina quarter-final at Lansdowne Road.

A few decades ago Charles de Gaulle, in a moment of frustration, wondered how he 'could possibly be expected to unite a country which has 265 different kinds of cheese'. It has been a bit like that in French rugby in recent times, a case of too many cooks spoiling the broth, to adopt an even more apt Anglo-Saxon metaphor to illustrate the over-abundance of coaches and off-the-field policy-makers and the lack of a clear chain of command on the field. To describe them as being like the cowboy in the Old Wild West, galloping off

in all directions, would certainly be appropriate for France and their eccentricities in last season's Five Nations and in their progress to the RWC 1999 quarter-finals from what was the easiest pool in the tournament. The two times Five Nations Grand Slam champions in 1997 and 1998 had a woeful 1999, losing their two home games for the first time in 42 years. The only win – 10-9

The French rugby public would have been hoping that Pierre Villepreux and France's coaching-management team could get their message across to their players in time.

against Ireland – could easily have been a loss and earned, instead, a wooden spoon as David Humphreys missed a last-kick-of-the-match penalty chance. And the southern hemisphere tour in the summer preceding the World Cup was a disaster – the French beaten by Tonga, New Zealand 'A', and the All Blacks by 54-7.

Nor was French flair all that visible as they won their three Pool C ties. They beat Canada 33-20, not the most positive of results; managed an easy 47-13 win over the disappointing Namibia; and had a tough encounter with Fiji before winning 28-19. Nothing to cause bonfires to be lit on the hilltops, but it was enough to bring them to Dublin after an invaluable eight days' rest to take on the mainly still amateur Argentina, who only four days beforehand had shocked the Irish in Lens. So here were the stuttering French, favourites to win through to the semi-finals. Would that coaching-management team of

Below: An Argentinian supporter gets behind her team in Dublin. The Irish, defeated by the Argentinians in the play-off round, also took the courageous Pumas to their hearts.

France's fly half Christophe Lamaison kicks over the head of the Puma captain, Lisandro Arbizu. Lamaison's right boot was responsible for 22 of his side's 47 points.

former greats, Jean-Claude Skrela, Pierre Villepreux and Jo Maso, sort out their different brands of cheese in time? The omens for advancing very much further were not great. Villepreux, on the eve of the Dublin quarter-final said: 'The method we play to is good. The problem is the players do not know how to use it.' Certainly the French have the very greatest of the game's illustrious former players as advisors. The question all France was asking was: Were the great players great communicators?

The arrival of the Argentinians in Dublin was brimming over with irony. First, they patiently awaited their time to check into their west Dublin hotel, the secluded Georgian Finnstown House, because the Irish, who had left their gear there, had to pack and vacate their headquarters – hurriedly. And then came the news that the Pumas' coach, Alex Wyllie, the man who had quietly

masterminded the victory at Lens, was remaining in Ireland to coach the north Dublin side Clontarf. And then came the supreme irony – the announcement by the Irish Rugby Football Union that Lansdowne Road was booked out for the presumed Ireland-France quarter-final had to be slightly rephrased. Expensive match tickets were being returned. And the many pubs in the vicinity of Lansdowne Road which had banners proclaiming: 'No tickets? See the match here on Wide Screen' had to perform a quick and discreet removal job.

As it happened, the Irish crowd had late second thoughts, and the ground, if not as packed as it would have been had it been Ireland v France, was fairly full,

Following pages: Puma full back Ignacio Corletto manages to offload to Lisandro Arbizu as French left wing Christophe Dominici makes his presence felt.

with a large contingent of French supporters whose 'Allez les Bleus' was as dominant as if the match was at the Stade de France instead of the little green spot in the heart of Dublin. And everybody got their money's worth with a rip-roaring, all action, intensely competitive game proving the best and most entertaining so far in the cup.

Even if France were tending to stagger their way through the competition, few could see any result but the French advancing to the semi-finals. Apart from any other considerations, hadn't they had eight days' rest before their Dublin engagement and weren't the Pumas having their third game in eight days? And when France led 17-0 after a mere 11 minutes, the writing – in fluent French – was on the wall. And the hullaballoo from the French supporters got louder and louder, and their 'greeting' of an Argentinian penalty attempt ten minutes into the game would have evoked envy from a crowd in the old days at the Stade Colombes. As it happened, the trend of affairs, subsequently, ensured a fair reduction in decibels from the French until the later stages of this enthralling match.

There were ominous signs from the start for Argentina. After three minutes their scrum collapsed, and the quietly competent Christophe Lamaison knocked over the penalty goal. Then in the seventh minute came the first French try. Centre Richard Dourthe made the initial half-break, and No. 8 Christophe Juillet gave the scoring pass to full back Xavier Garbajosa, who had a clear passage to the Pumas' line to touch down behind the posts. Lamaison duly converted, a further instalment in his series of nine successful place-kicks out of ten – five conversions and four penalty goals – for a personal contribution of 22 points. Then in the eleventh minute came a classic display of all the old French style and instinctive grace. French élan at last. Argentina's blind-side flanker, Santiago Phelan, charged down a Lamaison drop-out from the 22, but the ball rebounded to lock Abdelatif Benazzi, who passed right to flanker Olivier Magne, one of the best players on the pitch. His super speed eluded the defence and his pass to wing Philippe Bernat-Salles enabled the latter to score at the posts. As Lamaison converted and

French loose forwards past and present on the rampage. Ex-back-rower Abdelatif Benazzi, now at lock, sets off with No. 8 Christophe Juillet and flanker Olivier Magne.

Above: Flying right wing Philippe Bernat-Salles, who along with Xavier Garbajosa scored two tries in the match for France, celebrates a touchdown in style.

the scoreboard registered 17-0, the Marseillaise rang out over the grey autumnal Dublin afternoon. Vintage song. Vintage French play. But if the French team, or indeed the Irish spectators, believed all this was a cue for Argentina to lie down and accept their fate they could not be more mistaken. From then on, until the last quarter, when the mainly amateur Pumas ran out of puff, this was one heck of a game. And the neutrals – the Irish who were humiliated at Lens – got behind Argentina, the brave and utterly committed underdogs. The French could not repeat any stylish back play for the rest of the first half.

Midway through that half that irrepressible little scrum half, Agustin Pichot – surely one of the stars of the World Cup – beat two French defenders, going over from a close-in scrum, and when out-half Gonzalo Quesada converted and added a penalty goal a couple of minutes

Puma stand-off Gonzalo Quesada, one of the goal-kicking sensations of the tournament, puts his meticulous technique into action and sends the ball goalwards.

later, a mere seven points was the deficit. Then a stroke of fortune for France. Emile Ntamack, that gifted back, charged down a kick from the Argentinian captain and centre, Lisandro Arbizu. The ball bounced in Ntamack's favour and he romped over for a touchdown. Lamaison converted, and it was 24-10 to France. Lamaison added a penalty goal to make it 27-10, but the remaining minutes of the half were Argentina's. Arbizu got a measure of revenge on Ntamack by beating him on the outside for a fine try, and Quesada converted and added a penalty goal. The half-time break had the score poised at 27-20.

Argentina battled fiercely on the resumption, and the crowd got behind them with roar after roar of support. Penalties from Quesada and Ignacio Corletto, the full back, had France only 30-26 ahead going into the last 15 minutes. Alas, that is when Argentina, feeling the effects of their spate of recent matches, ran out of stamina. France dominated the tired warriors in the last ten minutes, and Lamaison kicked a penalty goal and converted late tries by Bernat-Salles and Garbajosa. France advanced, 47-26, to the semi-final, the only one of the northern hemisphere sides to survive.

As he left the field just before the end, that superb scrum half Agustin Pichot received a huge ovation from the crowd. And let it be recorded that the French supporters joined wholeheartedly in the applause. Never, I think, has a visiting player to Lansdowne Road been accorded such an acclamation. Afterwards Pichot said: 'I'll not forget that for years.' Both teams were applauded off the ground, the Pumas particularly so, and they went around the ground, clapping and acknowledging their rapport with the crowd.

'Bravo, Argentina,' was Jean-Claude Skrela's first remark at the after-match press conference. And Argentina, who had won only a single game in nine World Cup ties in 1987, 1991 and 1995, returned home with heads high from RWC 1999. As for France, the big question as they departed Dublin for their semi-final tilt at the All Blacks was: Would they manage to get their fromage together at last?

French skipper Raphael Ibañez looks mightily relieved and the rest of his team look exhausted as the final whistle blows on a wonderful World Cup quarter-final.

for **discounted** online **airfares**...

wing forward

www.airnet.co.uk

Book direct with Airline Network and save up to 60% on
discounted scheduled flights plus online hotel booking and car rental.

FLY THE NET

USA · CANADA · AUSTRALIA · NEW ZEALAND · FAR EAST · EUROPE · WORLDWIDE

Quarter-Final

New Zealand v Scotland

Alan Lorimer

There was never any serious doubt that New Zealand would progress to the semi-finals of the 1999 Rugby World Cup. Anyone who disputed this notion had only to refer to rugby records, which reveal that Scotland have never, ever beaten New Zealand. The Murrayfield meeting between the two countries was the third time that Scotland had faced the All Blacks in a World Cup quarter-final, and in the event it was to be the Scots' best showing against the New Zealanders. Four years ago Scotland, after a brave and, one has to say, enterprising display, were eventually swamped by 48 points to 30, as New Zealand warmed up for their demolition job on England in the semi-final at Newlands.

The 1999 All Blacks looked an even better side. Stand-off Andrew Mehrtens, in the opinion of the All Black coach, John Hart, was playing the best rugby of his life, while elsewhere in the back line there was a plenitude of pace. Against them was a Scotland team brilliantly coached by Jim Telfer and his assistants John Rutherford and Hugh Campbell and supported by a fired-up Scottish crowd who had gone against the grain of their presbyterian culture by turning out in their thousands for this Sunday evening match.

Gary Armstrong, the Scotland captain, confessed afterwards that he had not experienced a crowd atmosphere like it since the 1990 Grand Slam. Ian McGeechan, taking over from Jim Telfer as Scotland coach at the end of the World Cup, talked about the theatre atmosphere of a night match, magnified somehow by the steady rain that fell during the game.

Before the match, the talk in the Scotland camp had been about how to contain the giant Jonah Lomu, the stopping of whom makes the job of a bomb-disposal expert seem lower down the list of dangerous occupations. The Tongan-born Lomu, it will be recalled, caused mayhem in defences during the 1995 World Cup, the worst carnage being against England in the semi-final game at

Stand-off Andrew Mehrtens kicked two penalties and two conversions and set up Jeff Wilson's try. Just before half-time, though, he was forced to retire with a leg injury.

The Scotland team face up to the New Zealand haka and the wet weather at Murrayfield. Considering the atrocious conditions the quality of the rugby on view was remarkable.

Newlands, when reputations were cast aside as the massive All Black wing romped in for four tries.

Scotland, who, as mentioned, played New Zealand in the quarter-finals, did not escape either, as Craig Joiner, who had the unenviable task of marking Lomu, will testify. Again, when Scotland played New Zealand at Carisbrook in the first of two Tests on the Scots' 1996 tour, Lomu brushed aside Joiner to score one of his hallmark tries. Fortunately for Scotland Lomu picked up an injury and had to sit it out for the second Test.

As though issuing instructions on how to corner a man-eating tiger, Scotland coach Jom Telfer had advised: 'We have to close down his space, we have to crowd him out, we have to turn him, and we have to make sure that there are at least three or four players going for him.' On the day, the Scotland players took Telfer's final piece of advice to heart and made sure that for the most part there was a swarm of potential tacklers closing in on the target

whenever Lomu was in possession of the ball. As events turned out it was New Zealand's other wing, Tana Umaga, who proved to be the more dangerous of the two All Black wingers by scoring two first-half touchdowns to help his side to a 25-3 half-time lead. Umaga's first after just 12 minutes, and following a penalty goal by Mehrtens, was reward for New Zealand pressure, but three minutes later when Jeff Wilson ran in a try from Mehrten's counterattack after Gregor Townsend had failed to find a touch it seemed Scotland were set to suffer a big defeat.

A second Mehrtens penalty to add to his two earlier conversions confirmed that the New Zealand stand-off was in top kicking form, but that was to be his final shot at goal. Just before half-time Mehrtens suffered a leg injury and could not attempt the conversion of Umaga's second try, created by wonderful fingertip passing by Wilson and Christian Cullen. Wilson was given the touch-line kick but was off target.

Right wing Tana Umaga may not hit the headlines as often as Jonah Lomu, but his two tries in the first half at Murrayfield put New Zealand on the road to victory.

Scotland await a New Zealand conversion attempt. The All Blacks 25-point first-half blitz seemed to presage a massacre, but the Scots rallied to win the second half 15-5.

Scotland's only first-half points had come from a penalty goal by Kenny Logan, but the Scots had shown enough signs of enterprising play in the first 40 minutes to suggest that they might not be a spent force. That was confirmed in the opening exchanges of the second half, Scotland eventually profiting from some choice possession with a dropped goal by Townsend.

No New Zealand performance is complete without a try from Lomu, and when the powerhouse wing was put in the clear by a long pass from Josh Kronfeld, the score was inevitable. John Hart remarked afterwards: 'That was the new Jonah Lomu we saw. He's now prepared to take his

Jonah Lomu slides home, having taken Cameron Murray on the outside. Murray later had his revenge, selling the All Black an outrageous dummy before crossing to score.

Above: Hooker Gordon Bulloch celebrates Scotland's first try, registered by flanker Budge Pountney, who still lies concealed beneath the press of bodies.

man on the outside.' Lomu's try atoned for an earlier missed scoring opportunity, when the big man lost possession of the ball with the line at his mercy. Tony Brown, replacing Mehrtens, missed the conversion; even so New Zealand were comfortably in the lead 30-6.

Scotland, however, urged on by the huge home support – the first time the Scottish public had really got behind their team – sensed they were forcing their way back into the game. When Logan made an infield run that all but brought a score, the Scots' forwards set up a series of rucks on the New Zealand line that ended with flanker Budge Pountney being driven over for a try, coolly converted by Logan.

Budge Pountney tries to lay his hands on New Zealand scrum half Justin Marshall. Pountney's 67th-minute try was his first for his country.

Doddie Weir, who partnered Scott Murray in the Scotland second row, tucks the ball under his arm and prepares to take on New Zealand's Norm Maxwell (4).

Then, going into injury time Scotland struck again. Ironically it was one of Scotland's Kiwis, Martin Leslie, who set up the score with an interception. When Leslie realised he did not have the pace to outrun the defence, he looked for support and found Cameron Murray steaming up ready to take the pass. Murray, too, seemed to be closed in, but an outrageous dummy by the Scotland wing to Lomu deflected the defence sufficiently for Murray to race over for the Scots' second try. The match ended 30-18 to New Zealand, but Murray's score mitigated the pain of defeat and brought pride back to the Scottish game. Twenty-four hours after the game Telfer reflected: 'The Scotland team did us proud. This was a great advert for Scottish rugby. All the best characteristics of Scots came out – the bravery in defence and the refusal to give up. Never have I seen a second-half display like that from a Scotland team.' Well though Scotland had performed, the

All Black fly half Tony Brown, on for the injured Andrew Mehrtens, feels the force of Scotland's Jamie Mayer, as the centre tries to punch a hole in New Zealand's midfield.

perennial premise of southern hemisphere superiority remained a perpetual truth. It has everything to do with the intensity of the rugby south of the equator, a point on which John Hart remarked succintly: 'People tend to underestimate the difference in intensity between the Tri-Nations series and the Five Nations Championship.'

Above all, this match at Murrayfield will be remembered by the Scotland fans as the final curtain for Gary Armstrong. In an emotionally charged atmosphere at the end of the quarter-final, Armstrong made known to his team-mates what he had already communicated to Telfer. After the match Telfer paid tribute to the retiring Scotland captain: 'He's one of the bravest players I've ever seen. He should have been a flanker, but he wasn't big enough. I haven't seen a player who epitomised the Scottish character more,' said Telfer, who, himself, was departing from the international stage.

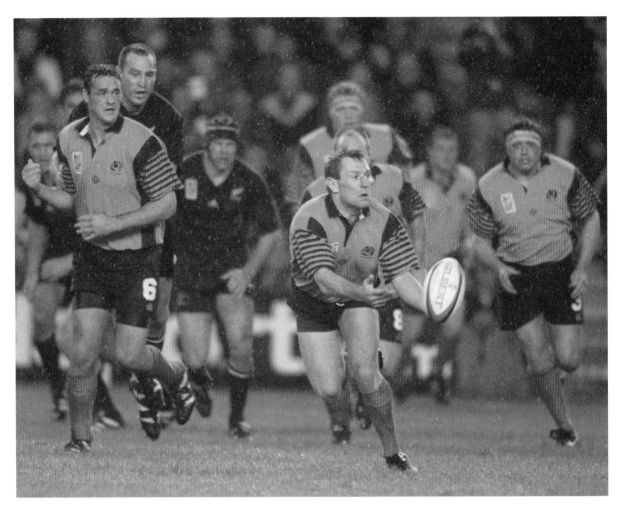

Almost the end of the road for one of Scottish rugby's great players. Gary Armstrong confirmed at the end of the match that he was retiring from international rugby.

Armstrong, whose understated Scottish character has been of enduring appeal, spoke of his side as the best Scotland team he had been involved in, and at least bowed out on a high. Scotland had won the second half 15-5. That was surely a permanent memento for Armstrong to take with him, even if New Zealand had once again beaten Scotland. It was a night, too, when Alan Tait and Paul Burnell announced their retirements from international rugby. For Tait it was the end of a phenomenal career in which he had represented Scotland in the 1987 and 1999 World Cups and in between the Lions in 1997 and Great Britain at Rugby League, an achievement few Scottish sportsmen can possibly match. 'Alan brought to the Union game tremendous experience. His strength was defence and being able to run good angles. He was a very positive

force in the Scottish team. He was a great servant to the Scottish game,' added Telfer.

Burnell, born in Edinburgh, was also a Lion (1993) and like Armstrong shared in the Scots' 1990 Grand Slam and the 1999 Five Nations win. A solid scrummager, Burnell was never given the credit he truly deserved, but his longevity, which added up to just 50 caps, was the final epitaph of his true worth.

For Scottish rugby, the 1999 World Cup quarter-final was the end of the road, but in another sense it was the beginning of another that pointed to a more hopeful future to replace the divisions of the past. For New Zealand it was the inevitable progression to the semi-final, and further proof that southern hemisphere rugby is still ahead – for the moment anyway.

And the final curtain, too, for another of the greats of the Scottish game. Jim Telfer says farewell to the Murrayfield faithful as he bows out as Scotland's director of rugby.

Telephone

Taxi

Airport

Bank

HSBC. It's a sure sign that you're dealing with a world-class financial services organisation.

We've been around for more than 130 years. Now we're in 79 countries and territories, serving over 20 million customers.

Those are the numbers. But it's our integrity and common sense solutions that you can truly count on.

Wherever you are in the world, wherever you are in your life, HSBC will be there for you.

HSBC

YOUR WORLD OF FINANCIAL SERVICES

Issued by HSBC Holdings plc

Semi-Final

Australia v South Africa

Mick Cleary

All eyes on the goal. With no time left on the clock, Jannie de Beer steps up and strokes the equalising penalty between the posts, as Joost van der Westhuizen looks on.

The rain lashed down from the sky, the winds howled as if the apocalypse was about to pay a visit, and down below on the sodden Twickenham turf, Springbok fly half Jannie de Beer lined up a penalty kick at goal that had just a tiny bit riding on it. The kick was into the teeth of the gale, from wide out on the right, about 38 metres from goal. Almost eight minutes of injury time had spun by, even though the official electronic board had signalled that only two minutes were to be added on. The nails on both benches had been eaten down to the roots when the giant mitt of Australian back-row substitute Owen Finegan was spotted by referee Derek Bevan, scrabbling for the ball at the bottom of a ruck. Whistle, penalty and a huge intake of breath from the 70,000 crowd.

De Beer, a modest fellow, moved towards the ball as if he were idling to the first tee of a Sunday morning round of golf. He lined it up. Surely the hero of the quarter-final, the man whose record five dropped goals had helped to fell England, was not about to strike again? He was. If the little voice of doubt were whispering that this could be the failure which caused South Africa to lose their first ever match in a World Cup, then he betrayed no sign of it. The ball flew between the posts. The Springboks had somehow salvaged the game and extra time it was.

We have long associated Springbok rugby with divine intervention. The first collective act of the 1995 World

Wallaby centre Tim Horan, debilitated by illness, although you wouldn't have known it, tries to elude the desperate grasp of Springbok flanker André Venter.

Cup-winning side was to drop to their knees in a huddle at Ellis Park to give thanks to God on that glorious afternoon four years ago. De Beer had paid homage to the Lord after his 34-point match-winning performance against England. Against Australia, the 'Boks were on the back foot for long stretches of this enthralling heavyweight tussle. Yet they hung in there. Their bodies must have been screaming with exhaustion, but their spirit never gave way. Deep, deep within lies the conviction that they should never be beaten. Deep within their souls, they believe that celestial eyes are watching over them.

The Australians are a great study in sporting excellence. On the exterior they are all laid-back, easy-going, down-to-earth blokes, typical Aussies just happy to have ball in hand and a field to play on. It's all nonsense of course. They are as driven and tough and resilient as any South African or Kiwi. Sure, rugby may not affect the sporting heartbeat of the nation as it does in both South Africa and New Zealand, but it sure as hell matters on a personal level. Do not be fooled by external appearances – they will tell you nothing. You only had to listen to the tales of the two key figures from this game to realise that theory does not always match up with reality.

Wallaby centre Tim Horan, who was without doubt man of this remarkable match, spent most of Friday in bed. He'd watched a movie at Burnham Beeches Hotel on Thursday evening, then hit the sack. He woke at 6 a.m. with vomiting and diarrhoea. The doctor was alerted, medication prescribed and Horan went back to bed where he slept until five o'clock that evening. He took a walk, ate one piece of toast and retired to bed. By the next morning he was just about passed fit, although Rod Kafer was told to pack his kit and be ready to play. Two more pieces of toast went down and that was it. On the 45-minute coach drive to Twickenham, Horan sat by the toilet.

Some three hours later, in the 74th minute of the match, Horan finally waved the white flag. He had given one of the great displays of centre-threequarter play. Springbok flanker André Venter, normally such an impenetrable force, and who had given England not a centimetre the week before, was beaten not once but three times across the gain line, Horan foxing him with his power, his balance and his eye for the gap. 'I seriously

Above: That man Horan again, this time tearing past South Africa's Percy Montgomery. Meanwhile, John Eales and Toutai Kefu try to keep up and offer their runner support.

thought about pulling out on Friday evening,' said Horan, who had to receive medication at the interval for stomach cramps. 'It was adrenalin that kept me going. My legs were jelly by the time I came off.' Even the Australian medical team were taken aback by Horan's resilience. 'That sort of bug would have forced a normal citizen into bed for at least two days,' said Wallaby doctor John Best. 'He showed enormous courage. He functioned at a very strong mental level.'

Enter another Australian hero. Stephen Larkham made his mark in an entirely different fashion. The scores were tied at 21-21 and only seven minutes of extra time remained when Larkham took a ball from George Gregan just inside the South African half. A lazy swing and the ball set off to the right of the posts. About 22 metres out it began its curl inwards, drawn as if by a magnet towards the white sticks. Larkham had scored a superb dropped goal, and the Springbok resolve wilted. Even their inner man, battered yet defiant, realised that the game was up. Matt Burke was to add another penalty goal, his eighth of the afternoon, to confirm victory.

The scourge of England in Paris, Jannie de Beer, missed four dropped goals in all. He struck one, in the 51st minute, to bring the scores to 12-12. He also landed six penalty goals. There was never more than six points between the teams at any stage. De Beer had practised his

dropped goals faithfully before the England game. And Larkham? 'A few of the guys did a lot of practising last week,' said Larkham. 'I might have had five or six kicks in training. I think I got one of them. Actually I don't think I've ever landed a drop goal in senior rugby at any level. Tim Lane [assistant coach] mentioned the possibility just before we went out for extra time. When I got the ball I looked up and saw just a wall of South Africans in front of me. The ball was in an awkward position and I thought there was no chance here.'

This game is still about character and talent and sheer dogged will. Larkham, who had missed ten months of rugby with a series of injuries, took a heavy blow to the knee in the fourth minute. There was internal bleeding. 'I had to keep the leg moving or it would seize up,' said Larkham. 'It was sore after every kick.'

There were other Australian heroes on a dramatic afternoon. John Eales, another with a smile on his face and steel in his heart, was a real force in the line out and around the field. His sense of the ball and awareness of

Opposite: Springbok prop Os du Randt tries to hand off Australian livewire George Gregan, who seems to have no intention of letting go of his man.

Above: Not elegant, perhaps, but effective. All-round master footballer John Eales kicks downfield as 'Bok No. 8 Bobby Skinstad attempts to charge down.

space are without equal. We may marvel at the subtle touch of a Seve or Sergio on the golf course, or a George Best in his pomp, but watch Eales in the line out. With elbows flying and bodies bumping, Eales is a study in serenity. His eye is sharper than anyone's, and his jump will meet with the throw precisely at the designated spot. He also has soft hands that adjust at the last split second to cradle the ball. He's not bad round the field either.

The scrap between the two scrum halves, George Gregan of Australia and Springbok captain Joost van der Westhuizen, was worth the admission price alone. How Gregan tackled and harried. How van der Westhuizen strove to break free. Gregan almost stole the honours in the 71st minute. In one of the few sustained sequences of the afternoon, the Wallabies went through eight phases, carefully working the ball to the right corner. One more phase, one more blast forward from the pack, and there's the gap. Gregan lunges for it and appears about to touch down. As he stretches he is hit by a double tackle from wing Pieter Rossouw and, yes, that man Joost. No

Left: Springbok captain Joost van der Westhuizen is held up by Matt Burke and David Giffin. Van der Westhuizen typified the South African attitude of 'No surrender'.

surrender. There was a big game too from Australia's Tongan-born No. 8, Toutai Kefu, whose blasting charges into the South African midfield kept the 'Boks on the back foot and helped nullify the threat of de Beer's boot.

'We have a lot of respect for the Australians,' said Springbok coach Nick Mallett. 'It was easy to go into the changing rooms and congratulate them. It was a fantastic game of rugby – hard and fast. Larkham is a lovely footballer. I'm not sure even he really considered the drop goal. He just put it down and gave it a big hoof.' Australian coach Rod Macqueen didn't even watch de Beer's last kick. 'I was busy making notes for extra time,' said Macqueen. 'It was a game of chess out there, moving one way and then the other. It was terrific watching two sides parrying each other, looking for a weakness.'

Following pages: As the rain and gloom descend on Twickenham, Matt Burke sends home the penalty that made the final score Australia 27, South Africa 21.

It ended 27-21 – no tries, but it did not matter. There was an intensity about the occasion and enough theatre in the denouement to satisfy any spectator. They had come in their thousands from South Africa, seven specially chartered Jumbos landing at Heathrow that morning. They filed out into the Twickenham evening with sadness in their hearts. Their reign as world champions was over.

Below: Sweetly timed. Stephen Larkham registers his first international dropped goal in injury time in a World Cup semi-final, and wins the game for Australia.

International traveller

travels well worldwide

Scottish & Newcastle
INTERNATIONAL LIMITED

Tel: +44 (0)131 528 2000 Fax: +44 (0)131 528 2315

New Zealand v France

Bill McLaren

I n four World Cup tournaments and some 42 years of rugby coverage, I cannot recollect a match of such substantial enthralment, extraordinary physical output and complete disregard of the betting odds as France's incredible performance in showing the door to the mighty All Blacks before an enraptured 72,000 capacity audience at Twickenham, who reacted to the magical events placed before them with all the unfettered enthusiasm they usually reserve for the pride of England. No one gave France a chance against New Zealand, who, although they had lost the second half of their Murrayfield quarter-final joust with Scotland by 15-5, looked capable of carrying all before them for a repeat of their 1987 inaugural tournament success. On that occasion they had beaten France in the final by 29-9, and the odds suggested

they would do the same again. After all, had not the All Blacks put France to the sword 54-7, and by seven tries to one, in Wellington just four months previously? There had also been newspaper stories of dissension within the French squad, and, in addition, France had lost the services of their orchestrator Philippe Carbonneau and of one of the great loose-head props in Christian Califano.

Did the All Blacks subconsciously take victory for granted? It would be most unlike them to do so. Certainly their coach, John Hart, worried prior to the game that on their day and with all guns ablaze the French were

Free and clear. No one can catch France's powerpack left wing, Christophe Dominici, as he flies across the Twickenham turf to score France's second try.

capable of running up a score against anyone, especially as even their captain, Raphael Ibañez, had come under fire as having led France to a Grand Slam in 1998 and a Wooden Spoon in 1999.

The match had everything, including French resolve to take on the All Blacks in all of their strong points – forward drive and dynamic rucking with scant regard for personal well-being; thunderous tackling, especially in midfield; rumbling, rolling mauls with ball hidden and scant regard for the law in relation to blocking off in front of the ball carrier; and intent to spin the ball wide, wherever the requisite platform had been set up. There was, too, a clear decision on the part of every French player to take whatever 'big hits' might come their way and just get up and take some more. It was a big plus for France also that they proved superior in ball retention.

There had been, quite rightly, much praise of the New Zealand back four – Jeff Wilson, Christian Cullen, Tana Umaga and Jonah Lomu. Each was a lethal ball carrier with burning pace on top, and between them they had

already amassed 104 tries in major internationals. Clearly, putting the handcuffs on those four had to be a French priority. On the day, however, it was France who created most of the crucial incisions, none more so than chunky little fireball Christophe Dominici, who popped up all over the paddock like an animated meerkat and on one occasion made a quite astonishing side-stepping run over 40 metres, the prelude to the try by Christophe Lamaison. It was hard to imagine a New Zealand defence, who regard leaked tries as they would family bereavements, so comprehensively embarrassed by one twinkle-toed little Frenchman, but Dominici's run past some five opponents simply opened the way for quick ruck delivery to send Lamaison sauntering over for a remarkable score.

The game proved a tour de force for Lamaison. Seldom can a makeshift stand-off have created such an impact in the most testing circumstances. Apart from his judicious use of the boot to create positions that kept the batteries of his forwards topped up, he weighed in with 28 points from a full house – one try, four conversions, three penalty goals and two dropped goals. He also did his full share of the torpedo work in midfield that proved such a key ingredient in the French strategy. Time and again, Tana Umaga, Christian Cullen, slippery as a wet haddock,

Full house for Lamaison. The French stand-off, challenged here by All Black skipper Taine Randell, registered a try, four conversions, three penalties and two dropped goals.

Above: French defenders wonder what hit them – Jonah Lomu has powered his way through five of them, including some mighty men, to score his first try of the afternoon.

Alama Ieremia, all 15st 10lbs of him, and Jeff Wilson had their legs scythed from underneath them. In most cases it was back to the old copybook style of tackling that had as its watchword the theory that even big and tricky men cannot go anywhere without their legs.

Lomu, as always, proved something of an exception. Sundry Frenchmen had a go at him, none shirking an unenviable obligation. Time after time they sank him. But on two famous occasions he proved just too much for them. He demonstrated swerve, hand-off, hip bumps and a form of fly swatting in escaping from no fewer than five opponents for his first try; in scoring his second, he showed he has lost none of the pace that once gave him a time of 10.8 seconds for 100 metres – all of which was another hint of his awesome power. Not surprisingly he set

Right: Here we go again. This time Lomu is too much for Bernat-Salles, Garbajosa and Galthié, as he cuts a swathe through France's defence for his second try of the game.

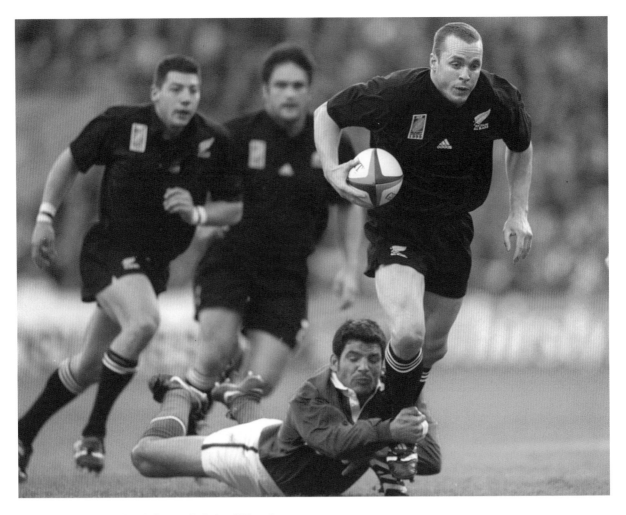

All Black centre Christian Cullen can't shake off French flanker Marc Lièvremont. Tenacious French tackling smothered the threat of New Zealand's midfield runners.

a new world record for a World Cup finals tournament by increasing his haul in RWC 1999 to eight tries.

Although no New Zealander made injuries an excuse for such a shattering experience, I wonder how much they did affect the All Blacks' display. Andrew Mehrtens had been doubtful with knee damage all week and, indeed, was listed as certain not to play right up until the day of the game. He was passed fit to play, yet he was not the Mehrtens who had drawn all-round praise during the tournament, even though he kicked six goals to take his points tally to 576 in just 38 Tests. His Garryowen punting was uncharacteristically vulnerable, he failed to provide a momentum target for his colleagues in pursuit, and there was no sign of that searching pace with which he had caught the Scots by surprise at Murrayfield. Tony

Brown was on the replacements bench yet was not introduced with a view to supplying an additional spark to New Zealand's attacking play.

There was, too, an injury to that dynamic flanker Josh Kronfeld. He is nicknamed the 'Otago Tornado' and recently he had been in his best sniffer-dog form as a constant presence at the main action points of the game, but early on against France he seemed dazed enough to suggest concussion. New Zealand did have a regular flanker on the bench in Andrew Blowers, who had played in 11 Tests, but Kronfeld stayed on. The injury, however, seemed to affect his contribution. Most times you can't help seeing Kronfeld, who covers the paddock like a niggly wolfhound. On this occasion, he didn't leave that kind of imprint, so that it was France's open-side flanker, Olivier Magne, who took all the honours in loose-forward play. Magne, like his high-scoring team-mate, Christophe Lamaison, wrote his name all over this epic encounter.

Right: All Black replacements Tony Brown (left) and Justin Marshall watch the unfolding drama from the bench. Marshall later got in on the action; Brown had to sit it out.

There was another injury factor which seemed to limit the effectiveness of the All Blacks' full back, Jeff Wilson. He had become New Zealand's top Test try scorer with 38, five of which had been registered in this World Cup, but now he was limping after being injured, and in the 60th minute he was beaten to the touchdown by Richard Dourthe, following a crafty diagonal punt from Lamaison, who thus exploited Wilson's wide positioning. It was sad for the New Zealand full back too that tactical misjudgment on his part had earlier proved costly. In the 56th minute he could have ignited Lomu but instead turned into a wall of French forwards who stole the ball. Scrum half Fabien Galthié hoofed the ball towards the left flank where the ever-alert Dominici latched on to it like a basketball star and scorched 40 metres for a thrilling try.

Below: The 'Otago Tornado', Josh Kronfeld, moves in on French No. 8 Juillet. By his usual standards, Kronfeld was subdued in this match, perhaps because of injury.

Following pages: Richard Dourthe raises his arm in celebration after having pounced on a finely placed kick ahead by Christophe Lamaison to score France's third try.

After a dramatic kick and chase from deep inside the French half, Philippe Bernat-Salles beats Jeff Wilson to the touchdown to score France's fourth try.

France's fourth try came in the 74th minute from a breakdown in a New Zealand attack deep in the French half. Umaga fumbled a pass, Lamaison hacked the ball forward, and Magne tore upfield after it. The All Black defence gained on Magne, but French flying machine Bernat-Salles arrived in the nick of time and shot past his team-mate at the line to touch down just ahead of Wilson.

This win was, perhaps, the greatest ever performance by a French side because it not only encompassed wonderful opportunism and blistering sequences of gorgeous team play – with their skill levels holding up even under the most physical of All Blacks defence – but because the French forwards took on their rivals with total commitment, not least their three big men: Abdelatif Benazzi, a giant of a motivator; Fabien Pelous, back after suspension and a thundering element throughout; and Olivier Brouzet, who replaced No. 8 Christophe Juillet after only 32 minutes and made a huge impact, particularly with the leap of a freshwater salmon in the line-out delivery from which Dourthe scored his try.

Did New Zealand err in preferring Byron Kelleher to Justin Marshall? In doing so they split the Canterbury pairing of Marshall and Andrew Mehrtens that had been so productive in their 27 Tests together. Kelleher, a 15-stone tough hombre from Otago, was liable to ask questions of France's fringe defenders and already had scored World Cup tries against England and Tonga. But against France he never looked like making a clean break. Marshall came off the bench but too late to impress his personality on the proceedings, although his long pass did set up an 80th-minute score for Jeff Wilson.

Referee Jim Fleming's final whistle blew with the score at 43-31, and France, having thus recorded their biggest ever score against the All Blacks in a Test, took a lap of honour, the audience who had been so royally entertained giving them a standing ovation. France and New Zealand really set fire to the 1999 Rugby World Cup and set a benchmark for international Rugby Union to follow – not least in the World Cup final at Cardiff's magnificent Millennium Stadium on 6 November.

The French do a lap of honour around Twickenham after they and New Zealand had produced one of the greatest contests ever seen at English rugby's headquarters.

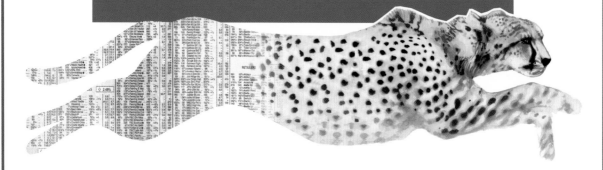

Third-Place Play-Off

New Zealand v South Africa

Eddie Butler

A nd so the two mightiest rugby nations of the twentieth century came to the Millennium Stadium on the eve of the twenty-first century for their showdown. But it was no title-settling sell-out in Cardiff. The patches of empty seats in the stands were an echo of earlier World Cup non-events in Murrayfield. The All Blacks and the Springboks came to decide merely who would have to pre-qualify for the next tournament. Such are the charms of the third-fourth play-off.

But it was still New Zealand against South Africa. As Joost van der Westhuizen said afterwards, when asked if the players had managed to motivate themselves for this game, 'For a game against the All Blacks? That is enough in itself. I did not have to worry.' But what about New

Springbok wing Stefan Terblanche is held by replacement back Pita Alatini and Jeff Wilson, who moved from full back to the wing for the second half.

Zealand? Word had travelled fast from the other side of the globe that the lynch mob was waiting back home. The ticker-tape parades had been cancelled, leaving a little whiff of scandal about who was going to pay for the presumption of organising them in the first place. Who was going to pay for the defeat against France? One way of keeping the mob at bay was to put on a feisty display and end on some sort of high note.

The note was not struck by either team. These two nations had never met before on neutral soil, but shock induced by the semi-finals had the players walking

through syrup rather than striding into history. There was the semblance of a rising climax, as the All Blacks gathered themselves for the assault that might yield their first try and win them the game, but their best move in the closing seconds ended with another hallmark gesture of this tournament. Referee Peter Marshall pointed at Royce Willis and gave that all too familiar signal that the tackled player had held on to the ball too long after the

tackle. On the big screens, the face of John Hart was cut up more and more frequently. These were cruel cuts.

The All Blacks kicked their penalties: six of them by Andrew Mehrtens. They nearly released Jonah Lomu once. The underused giant of '99 – how different from '95, when he was eventually the overworked star of the show – received one pass that gave him the half yard he needed to build up to full speed and power. He was brought down by

a neat tap-tackle from Stefan Terblanche. As for South Africa, they had three moments of magic, which meant that their World Cup, on balance, ended in a satisfactory way. No one could really be blamed for underachievement in the semi-final against the Wallabies. In that contest, which had lasted for one hundred and seven minutes, the Springboks had been edged out by the Wallabies and by the dropped goal of Stephen Larkham in particular.

Referee Peter Marshall steadies the front rows at a scrum. On the nearside for South Africa is Ollie le Roux, on for Os du Randt. Opposite him for New Zealand is Kees Meeuws.

Now it was a Springbok's turn once again to deliver a killer dropped goal. It did not come from Jannie de Beer, though. The fly half who had kicked five against England had made a marvellous gesture before the game, offering to stand down so that Henry Honiball might enjoy one last

The dropped goal is king! Percy Montgomery celebrates after landing one against the All Blacks. The Springbok full back dropped two goals in the game – one in each half.

outing before retirement from the Test stage. Honiball played with authority but it was not his boot that provided the golden moment. Instead it was Percy Montgomery's. The full back had had a difficult year, embroiled in all the politics that went with South Africa's build-up. Was the Western Province player a favourite of Nick Mallett? Why hadn't the coach brought back André Joubert? Montgomery delivered in Cardiff. In the first half, from five metres inside the New Zealand half, he dropped a goal that went between the posts via a huge rebound off the crossbar. In the second, when a single point separated the sides at 19-18, he repeated the dose from closer range, but with an All Black bearing down on him.

The dropped goal was a World Cup king. But what about a try? South Africa had not managed one against the Wallabies, and here the defences were just as

impregnable. The players on both sides may have been traumatised by their semis, but they can tackle ferociously on automatic pilot nowadays. What did suffer was their handling. This was a game littered with turnovers and knock-ons. But South Africa did score, courtesy of wing Breyton Paulse, who had not made the line-up for the Springboks' big games previously. He showed what his team might have been missing.

As had so often been the case, it took a kick to undo the defence. Paulse delicately chipped over the All Black threequarters and set off in pursuit. He won the first sprint, kicked ahead, seemed to have lost the second, but the ball squirted away from the covering Christian Cullen. Paulse was the first to react, turning and guiding the ball a bit messily over the line with hand and knee. The finish may have been untidy, but the 50 metres before that was flowing grace. Individual brilliance allied to pace.

The All Blacks could not quite find the one individual who might salvage something for them. The front row

Right: Electric Springbok wing Breyton Paulse, who replaced fellow speedster Deon Kayser for this game and whose try effectively separated the sides at the whistle.

thundered on to the bitter end, but out where the fast players lurked they could not find the co-ordination of old. Which meant that Lomu was generally starved of the ball. Christian Cullen sparkled on occasions but was hauled down by the second tier of tacklers. As was Tana Umaga. As was Jeff Wilson. The most skilled players in the All Black team – indeed, in the World Cup – ended up in the static midfield bog of a side suddenly without confidence.

The final whistle blew at 22-18 and the South Africans raised their arms. This game had meant something. But whether a Test match between the Springboks and the All Blacks would remain the defining rugby challenge of the twenty-first century had been called into question. The All Blacks would have to pre-qualify for the World Cup of 2003, to be held in their own land. The sound of the lynch mob travelled fast once more around the globe.

Below: A dispirited-looking New Zealand troop off the field after suffering their second defeat in a week. In the stands John Hart was preparing to announce his resignation.

Following pages: Breyton Paulse (14), Joost van der Westhuizen (9), André Venter (7) and Percy Montgomery (15) hail South Africa's passage to the 2003 finals.

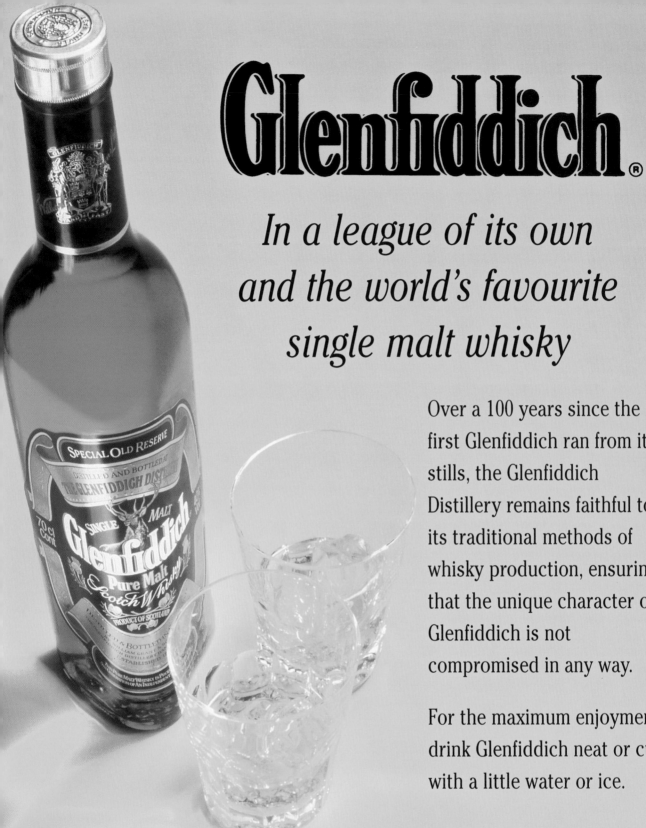

Glenfiddich®

In a league of its own and the world's favourite single malt whisky

Over a 100 years since the first Glenfiddich ran from its stills, the Glenfiddich Distillery remains faithful to its traditional methods of whisky production, ensuring that the unique character of Glenfiddich is not compromised in any way.

For the maximum enjoyment, drink Glenfiddich neat or cut with a little water or ice.

SINGLE MALT
Glenfiddich®
Scotch Whisky

Final
Australia v France
Bill McLaren

French lock Abdelatif Benazzi is left with his thoughts as the Wallabies withdraw after Ben Tune's try, Australia's first of the final, scored in the 65th minute.

There were those who predicted a dream final to the 1999 World Cup. France, after all, had blended opportunism and adventurism in creating the shock result of the entire tournament, the elimination of the hot favourites, New Zealand, in the semi-final. Surely there was no way that the French would damp down their bunsen burners just because it was a World Cup final. And everyone knew that Australia were capable of midfield wizardry, oftimes involving the pattering pugnacity of Tim Horan, the player of the tournament. Such a fusion was bound to present before an enthralled 72,500 audience in the Millennium Stadium in Cardiff an amalgam of high skill and daring that would light up the proceedings and that would be a credit to the great game.

It didn't turn out like that. Perhaps it was the occasion that induced a mood of caution. Perhaps it was the strength in the tackle and the total commitment to defence chores that, in the main, kept the door shut for fully an hour. After all, the Wallabies had reached the final having conceded just one try – and that curiously to one Juan Grobler of the USA. Nor had the French exactly left their door open all that often, with the concession of under two tries per match. Perhaps it was the heavy state of the pitch, despite the care in preparation given by Ground Manager Tony Horne and his staff.

They came hoping that their heroes could cause an upset for the second week running, but sadly for them France were unable to recapture the magic of the semi-finals.

The Australians kept a close eye on Christophe Dominici after his performance against the All Blacks. Here George Gregan attempts to pull down the stocky winger.

There were occasional little flurries in the final of attractive interplay but few of the flowing ball transference moves that bring an audience to its feet amid thunderous applause. There was a lot of punting. Indeed there had been a great deal of punting in this World Cup, and both France and Australia contributed their shares. Happily the use of the big boot was tempered by some deft touches in the use of diagonals and little chips or grubbers into space behind the opposing defence line. Apart from re-popularising the dropped goal, this World Cup also had underlined the value of the chip kick ahead as a means of saving your midfield from too many so called 'big hits', whilst circumventing flat-lying defence lines frequently augmented by large, rough men from the frontal areas. There was the added advantage, if kicks were well placed, of forcing opposing defenders to turn and therefore of placing them in less profitable situations. At worst, they forced the opposition to punt for touch with subsequent benefit of the throw-in.

The Australians had done their homework. The use of videos of opponents in action has lessened the surprise element, which is sad in a way, especially as the set pieces of scrummage and line out have become so predictable. In any event, Rod Macqueen, Australia's coach, and his disciples clearly had noted that, in their victory over New Zealand, the French had made clever use of the attacking diagonal punt into the in-goal area that had spawned the crucial try by Richard Dourthe. Christophe Lamaison had chip-kicked onto a sixpence for that score. When he tried the same against the Wallabies he found that Ben Tune and his colleagues were alert and anticipatory.

The Australians also had noted the trickery at pace of Christophe Dominici that had led to the try against the All Blacks by Lamaison. Dominici was kept on short rations by the Wallabies, but when he did ignite, sometimes on the other flank, he was astutely policed out of any more deeds of derring-do. Even so, Dominici had proved a World Cup star turn as a smaller type who could shift.

The French have fallen in with the modern practice of playing two big men in midfield – Emile Ntamack and Richard Dourthe at 6ft 2ins and 15st 6lbs. They present quite a threat in taking ball at pace and in tackle power. Between them they have scored 27 cap international tries. But the Wallabies were wise to this threat, and it is testimony to their discipline and application in defence work that in the entire finals tournament they still conceded just the one try. The Australians also had taken

Big French centre Richard Dourthe and veteran Wallaby flanker David Wilson engage in some aerial manoeuvres as Stephen Larkham and Marc Lièvremont look on.

note of the explosive quality to the play of France's dynamic open-side flanker, Olivier Magne. He occasionally threatened in the final but was never allowed to break the shackles.

It also was a crucial element in Australian success to limit the amount of genuinely usable ball available to France's dangerous runners. Australian ball retention,

then, was secure, and, notably at restart kicks, John Eales, the Wallaby captain, gave an impressive display of high leaping and gathering-in that the French just didn't match. The Australian line out was profitable throughout

David Giffin and Abdelatif Benazzi, widely considered the forward of the tournament, contest a line out. Both sides were well supplied with capable line-out jumpers.

the tournament. Eales was astute in ringing the line-out changes, so that David Giffin gathered in his share, and Matt Cockbain also proved a dependable auxiliary provider. Not that Australia ever hinted at huge line-out superiority, for France started off with Fabien Pelous and Abdelatif Benazzi in the front positions and with a much underrated line-out specialist further back in Magne. Not only that, but French line-out potential was boosted by the substitution after 40 minutes of the giant Olivier Brouzet for Christophe Juillet that enabled Pelous to switch from lock to No. 8, in which berth he already had operated for France on 14 occasions.

The French were adept at slewing the scrummage on Australia's insertion, but little advantage was gained here and it was the French who fell foul of referee André Watson of South Africa for taking it down. Watson was taking charge of his thirteenth major international and he certainly has had easier games. He began to get just a teeny bit testy after several examples of preventing fair release at tackle points, the French being the more guilty. Once again French indiscipline hindered their effort, so much so that when their captain, Raphael Ibañez, who was leading them for the twenty-first time, asked for an explanation of their penalty concession, Mr Watson told him that if his players were going to keep on infringing he would simply have to keep on penalising them! That seemed fair enough, yet the French seemed prepared at times to risk giving away three points for a penalty rather than seven points for a converted try.

It clearly is hard on referees who do seek to encourage fluent, exhilarating contests only to be thwarted in that ambition by failure to play within the laws. The inability of the French to keep their mitts off the ball in rucks made for a fractured contest with too many stoppages. Mr Watson blew his whistle a lot, which rather cut across the theory that southern hemisphere referees are less strict as they see themselves as an essential part of the rugby entertainment industry. But as long as the referee keeps the advantage provisions in mind, there isn't a lot he can do but award penalities if players are illegally preventing fair and quick recycling. I didn't hear Mr Watson remind the captains that for three offences on the ground, a player can be dismissed. It was mildly surprising too that

Jason Little can hardly contain himself, and Ben Tune (in centre on ground) looks pretty happy too, as referee André Watson signals the latter's try in the right-hand corner.

he had to show a yellow card to the Australian captain, John Eales, a gentleman on and off the field. He showed one also to the French lock Fabien Pelous, who was in rumbustious form elsewhere. Perhaps had the sin bin been available there might have been less offending and more running and handling action.

In their back line, Australia had Stephen Larkham, something of a flair player and without the punt control of Lamaison. The Australians nonetheless accommodated the Larkham style into their general strategy, such was the explosive nature of Tim Horan's contribution and the direct physical dimension to Daniel Herbert's method. As back-up also was the blend in Australia's loose-forward trio, of whom Toutai Kefu had opportunities created for him for the kind of power surge that carried his special trademark, whilst David Wilson, a renowned sniffer dog of a flanker, frequently slowed up France's tackle ball and was at the heart of Australian intent to give the French only minimal, if any, time on the ball. Matt Cockbain, known affectionately to his colleagues as 'Biscuit', gave glimpses of the kind of demolition work that has given him

the reputation of a devastating 'hit man'. France's breakaway men were never so influential for all the potential threat held out by Magne. Larkham also had the guiding hand of George Gregan inside him, a Gregan carrying a protective instinct towards his young partner.

Rugby being very much of a momentum game the French failed to generate that kind of momentum continuity, partly because of their own transgressions and because the Australian defence framework proved so well co-ordinated and had at its core impressive weight of tackle. Clearly the influence of John Muggleton, the former Rugby League player, on Australian defence coaching had been highly beneficial.

One other aspect of the French game had lost some of its value. Whereas in the match against the All Blacks the French half-back link between Fabien Galthié and Christophe Lamaison had been dependable and productive, it developed an element of hesitation and indecision that proved costly against the Australians. Apart from uncertainty at times on Galthié's part as to where his partner was to be found, there also seemed to be a fractional delay in Galthié's pass delivery that heightened the pressure on his partner. Such delay can enable an opposing flanker predator to get that bit closer to his prey, and it said much for Lamaison's temperament, skill levels and focus that he kept his head above water throughout. Galthié had a wealth of experience from 30 caps, and he had some notable feats in defence, but when he was replaced by Stephane Castaignède the pace seemed to quicken, as the substitute proved fractionally sharper in his pass delivery.

Happily the forward battle had just one torrid sequence, when little Dominici, all 13 stones of him, decided to add his bulk to a pile-up situation which suddenly developed into a general punch-up. That, however, was the only bout of fisticuffs in the game, although it was sad that Australia's captain, John Eales,

At first it looked as though he was looking for support or didn't think he could make it, then he just went for it. Owen Finegan on his way to score Australia's second try.

seemed to be on the same wavelength as the New Zealand coach, John Hart, in suggesting that the French had been guilty of acts of foul play, including eye damage, that should have no place in the game. On television, Michael Lynagh said that something had to be done to eliminate such practice from the game, and Eales said after no-side that 'there were some things happening out there that we were not too happy about', then added that 'it is disappointing because they are such a good side that they do not have to play like that to be competitive'. ·

In one other area Australia have been well served throughout the tournament. The quality of their replacement players has been so high that the shape of Australia's game never was subject to change. Jason Little, now possessed of 66 caps, simply slotted into the threequarter line as to the manner born, and when that large citizen Owen Finegan was introduced against the French, his contribution was decisive. Firstly, when the sniping George Gregan explored the narrow side, Finegan was the linkman for the first try of the match by Ben Tune, who smashed through the tackles of Xavier Garbajosa and Raphael Ibañez. And it was the Gregan-Finegan alliance again that delivered the coup de grace to the French.

Well done, mate. Owen Finegan's team-mates rush to congratulate him, knowing that his try has put Australia out of France's reach and in sight of the World Cup.

Finegan benefited from a sweet little reverse pass from Gregan after, not for the first time, Eales had leapt like a freshwater salmon to provide the line-out ammunition. Finegan then charged at fully five knots past four astonished Frenchmen for the crucial try that put on to the Irish-Australian's face one of the widest grins imaginable!

As Matt Burke added the conversions of Tune's and Finegan's tries to his seven penalty goals, he topped the 500 points mark in internationals (509) and finished second, on 101, just one point behind the Argentinian stand-off Gonzalo Quesada (102), in the list of leading points scorers for the finals tournament. As for Finegan, modern talk now is about 'impact' players being introduced as substitutes in order, one assumes, to make a big impact. They don't come much bigger than that achieved by the near 18 stones Finegan.

The Wallabies might have had another try when Horan, having worked a neat scissors with Larkham, provided a cheeky little reverse feed to Joe Roff, who got over the French goal line but lost the ball in the act of putting it on the ground, the crucial tackle that time coming from Garbajosa, who, with his white hair, had all the appearance of a moving street lamp!

The French had their near things as well, notably whenever Lamaison used the chip kick. Once, after 15 minutes, he directed it to Magne, who sent Abdelatif Benazzi over for a touchdown which was disallowed because Magne's feed had been fractionally forward. On another occasion Lamaison steered his punt to ignite the

Above: Wallaby left wing Joe Roff eludes the outstretched hands of Emile Ntamack (12). Roff so nearly scored a third Australian try but lost the ball in the tackle on the line.

scorching pace of Philippe Bernat-Salles, but Matt Burke showed that he too could pick up his feet by getting to the ball just before the 'Pau Rocket'.

The final proved disappointing in that there wasn't nearly enough of the rippling type of interplay and daring surges from the deep that had lit up the France v New Zealand semi-final, but no one doubted that the most deserving squad had won the William Webb Ellis Trophy. The Australians had gone about their business quietly and without fuss. They took the sad injury withdrawals of Phil Kearns and Patricio Noriega in their stride, Richard

Left: A desolate Richard Dourthe at no-side. France, written off earlier in the cup, bore the hopes of the north in the later stages but could not overcome a strong Wallaby side.

Harry and Andrew Blades giving their scrummage a solid foundation, whilst the throwing of Michael Foley contributed to their line-out surety. And they had a first-choice side that had barely a weakness. Matt Burke is arguably the most complete full back in the world game, and their threequarter line is marked by physical presence and pace, with Tim Horan a class act. The Larkham-

Gregan link was sound, Gregan's sniping threats easing the pressure on his partner. And the pack responded to their popular captain, Eales, with a wonderful series of

For Australia, it's time to celebrate a second Rugby World Cup success. Skipper John Eales (facing camera) knows what it feels like – he was there last time, in 1991.

John Eales, captain of Australia, hoists high the William Webb Ellis Trophy at the Millennium Stadium, Cardiff, having been presented it by Her Majesty the Queen.

performances in which they provided a solid set-piece platform, some choice, quick delivery from subsequent phases and, of course, they covered the pitch like an orange blanket and tackled as if their lives depended on it.

France gave the 1999 World Cup its most thrilling contest, their defeat of New Zealand setting fire to the finals when that was most needed. But they were unable to recapture that momentum and dazzling interplay, their captain, Ibañez, claiming, 'we were less fresh'.

So the Wallabies with their victory by 35 points to 12 became the first to win the Rugby World Cup twice in repeating their success of 1991, both wins being achieved away from home, whilst the All Blacks (1987) and the South Africans (1995) were world champions on home territory. When John Eales received the William Webb Ellis Trophy from Her Majesty the Queen, the celebrations began in earnest and, in a sense, the world joined in because the world knew that those popular Australians were worthy champions.

Below: The Wallaby scorers (l to r), Matthew Burke, Ben Tune and Owen Finegan. Burke contributed seven penalties and two conversions; Tune and Finegan a try apiece.

A GREAT TEAM TO HAVE BEHIND YOU

We are proud to support the Rugby World Cup book

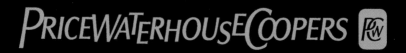

Retrospective

Four World Cups

Stephen Jones

From the outside, the only crucial change in Rugby World Cup since the pioneering first event in 1987 is that there were 16 competitors in the first three tournaments (New Zealand & Australia 1987, England & Europe 1991, South Africa 1995) and 20 in Wales & Europe 1999. Give or take the odd tweak to the format, give or take the fact that there is now an extended and often excellent programme of qualifying which galvanises the smaller nations of rugby's planet (whereas in 1987 you just had to turn up and play), it's all roughly the same.

And yet also it is profoundly different. Each World Cup has been a different type of experience, each has affected rugby in different ways. The beauty of these adventures at the rarefied summit of sport is that they spring surprises, fall into separate categories. Those of us who have had the good fortune to be asked to report on all four have found it a marvellously vivid, occasionally infuriating, but ultimately enriching experience, and the 1999 tournament evoked all those things.

To be in Australia and New Zealand in 1987 was to feel part of an expedition, was to feel yourself on some covered wagon prospecting in the Wild West, fearful of what you had started, fearful of what the unknown was going to do to everything you knew and loved. And we never needed to worry. As soon as that event started, everyone in rugby turned to his mate and asked why on earth it had taken so long. The answer was that the Home Unions and especially the English (who then held sway) felt that to hold a World Cup was the first step towards professionalism, that it would make rugby ever more serious. Well, it was and it did, for rugby was to double in size, in commercial appeal, in appeal to spectators; was to double and treble and quadruple the number of countries where it was played — the lot. And all because of the pioneers in 1987. Bless them.

The culture clashes were marvellous in those old days — Fiji playing a magnificent match against Argentina; Italy being thrashed in the opening game by the All Blacks, then pulling themselves together for a final pool victory. We first began to learn about those wondrously tough blokes from Canada; we rediscovered miracles when France beat Australia in the semi-final at Sydney's Concord Oval, a match then regarded as the greatest ever.

Even from that day you can draw a comparison to see how rugby has grown since 1987. There we had a semi-final of the World Cup involving Australia, the home team. The Concord Oval then took about 22,000 spectators, and it was not full. There must have been at least 200 empty seats. But two years later, when the British Lions went to Sydney to play the Wallabies, all three Tests were sold out, including two to the tune of 47,000 at the Sydney Football Stadium. Then, ten years after the first World Cup, over 90,000 people went to watch Australia play the All Blacks in Melbourne. It represents a staggering rise.

Cardiff hosts the Closing Ceremony of Rugby World Cup 1999. The tournament, the first of the professional era, left 'the impression of a growing sport in great heart'.

There was a parallel with 1999 back in 1987 because although the French reached the final, they found that they had expended most of their energy and passion in the semi, and lost convincingly to the All Blacks. The other parallel was the Brits played poorly, all qualifying for the quarter-finals, but only Wales were able to reach the semis, there to concede 49 points to a rampant New Zealand. Otherwise, it was a marvellous experience, new and fresh and wonderful in tone and temperament. It was in many ways the end of innocence, but it was preposterous to think that rugby could always exist in some kind of smug isolation, deeming itself immune to the world outside and all its realities.

In 1991, the old order was magnificently felled as Western Samoa won an epoch-making victory over Wales. The organisers dubbed 1991 the 'first real World Cup', in that there was qualifying, and there was a proper commercial programme, whereas deals had been done in Australia on the hoof. Disappointingly, the European Unions could not work out a formula to concentrate the tournament either in France or in the four Home Unions; that the tournament be so concentrated was the prime, overwhelming decision made in the post-mortem of 1987,

and it is the greatest disappointment of World Cup history for this observer that, South Africa 1995 apart, the organisers have failed to take their own advice, to the detriment of the tournament.

But those were heady days in 1991. You could see and feel rugby growing, feel it touching parts of British sporting hearts it had never touched before, feel it getting under the skin of the nation as good old England and Scotland powered their way to the semi-finals, and as Australia, wonderful ambassadors and a team loved deeply by the public in Europe for their play and behaviour, bore down on the other semi – and this after a vivid event in which Italy, Western Samoa, the USA, and Canada, and practically all the others had had their moments of glory. England reached the final by overpowering Scotland; Australia gloriously dumped the All Blacks; and then, with England meandering tactically, the Wallabies waltzed away with the crown in a final at Twickenham which still haunts great England forwards who felt that they had done enough to win. The Queen presented the Webb Ellis Trophy to Nick Farr-Jones, who handed it on down the line to the likes of David Campese, that peerless player and entertainer, Michael Lynagh, Phil Kearns, John Eales and the other heroes so well fashioned by Bob Dwyer, the coach.

But again, rugby had expanded, had banked a good few millions for global development, had revealed itself in all its maddening but vivid glory. It was silly even to waste the breath and say that it would never be the same again. Of course it wouldn't be.

Rugby found itself as only part of a wider experience in 1995 when we had what is probably, as far as these matters can be compared, the greatest of the World Cups to date. Rugby has always played a massive part in the wider landscape of South African life and especially in the apartheid period. Rugby had re-emerged from the boycott years as recently as 1992, and with President Mandela installed and with rugby trying to make reparations, then 1995, with the world looking on, was every bit as vital in South African life as it was in rugby's development.

Again, it was a triumphant few weeks of our lives, which ended with Mandela dancing on the podium as he presented the William Webb Ellis Trophy to Francois Pienaar, the statesman who had led the Springboks to the world title at the first attempt. For the moment at least, Pienaar and Mandela had touched and united their whole sad, bewitching, magnificent country. Alongside that

South African and Australian fans enjoy the World Cup atmosphere at Twickenham, while their champions prepare to do battle on the field in the first 1999 semi-final.

towering political and sociological significance, rugby's progress was rendered almost incidental.

But again, it was there all right. We now had the first anxieties that the gap between the haves and the have-nots of rugby in financial terms was becoming dangerously wide and that those romantic and compelling occasions when the smaller teams dumped the old giants, or even harried them to distraction in defeat, were becoming exceedingly few and far between; of the smaller nations, only the Samoans, not so fine a team as they had been in 1991, made the quarter-finals. Yet it was another tremendous rugby tournament, kicked on in the eye of the English audience when Rob Andrew dropped a goal for England in the dying moments to put them into the semi-finals and eliminate the reigning champions, Australia.

The semi-finals were something else. South Africa won through against France in Durban, fortuitously and on a pitch resembling a lake after monsoons. It was a staggering spectacle. And nothing compared to what happened on the following day, when New Zealand beat England with four tries from Jonah Lomu – already established as the most famous figure that the world of rugby had ever produced and as every defender's nightmare as the giant with the speed of a sprinter. The final, in which South Africa outlasted a New Zealand team drained by a rash of stomach upsets, was an anticlimax as a match, but not for its overwhelming significance. Rugby had never enjoyed such profile – and it was inevitable that soon after, it went professional.

By the time rugby's caravan came to Wales in 1999, new forces such as Spain, Uruguay and Namibia were hitched, and all three played wonderfully well. Marvellously, Samoa again beat Wales, though Wales showed encouraging signs of revival in the preamble to the tournament and proved that rugby fervency is alive and well by hosting the event with passion and by erecting the marvellous Millennium Stadium, easily the greatest rugby stadium in the world. Ultimately, the pressure of expectation hampered the Welsh performance, although they came as close as anyone to downing Australia.

It is true to say that by now the innocence had gone and the tournament was afflicted by some of rugby's new severities – poor administration, and play in which the defensive systems evolved by the massive athletes of the day held sway. Yet crowds were splendid everywhere bar in Scotland, and the party and fiesta which the event provides for the rugby public was as enjoyable as ever.

Argentina saw off Ireland for a place in the 1999 quarter-finals. They lost there to France but gave 'Les Bleus' plenty to think about, including this try by Lisandro Arbizu.

Canada and Samoa calmed the fears of the two-tier event, but Fiji and Argentina even more so, with Fiji testing France and England to the limit, and Argentina, reviving as the tournament progressed, eliminating Ireland. The history of the World Cup is most vivid when cultures clash and when shocks abound. The news that the International Rugby Board were to give major financial grants to the second tier of nations – the Pacific Islands, Argentina, etc – specifically so that they could prepare to take a major scalp was excellent.

Four World Cups, four fantastic experiences. It is sad that we are not yet at the point where the whole thing runs like clockwork, and a major administrative shake-up is still needed. But in general, they are wonderful. The old balance is there because we have had no drugs scandals, no ugly brawls, no controversies on the field which outlast the tournament itself. With the backdrop of rugby's great cathedrals, from the Millennium Stadium and the Stade de France and at all points east and west, the impression is of a growing sport in great heart. Four World Cups of sometimes dramatic differences and contrasts, but all have helped to take rugby to the forefront.

WING FORWARD

Stay ahead of the pack, call the Honda Information Hotline on 0345 585 570.

Player of the Tournament: Tim Horan

Andy Irvine

In 1995 the player of the tournament was Jonah Lomu, and it was very hard to argue with that, even though New Zealand did not win the World Cup. In 1999 I felt that the Australian centre Tim Horan was just as crucial to the Wallaby triumph as Lomu had been to the All Blacks team four years earlier. He was the focal point of their whole back division and took the pressure off his fly half, Stephen Larkham, who did not look a very commanding figure for a player in such an important position. The Wallabies looked to Horan to call the shots, and he is one of those gifted but rare specimens who seems always to do the right thing every time.

I can remember a similar player years ago when I was playing rugby and dinosaurs were running around on Mother Earth. He was the Irish and British Lions centre Mike Gibson. Tim Horan has come from the same mould. Like all great players in any sport, he always seems to have enough time and space to do what he wants to do, even in the claustrophobic pressure-cooker atmosphere of the knockout stages of a World Cup.

Horan was good when Australia won the World Cup at Twickenham in 1991, and at Cardiff in 1999 he was even better. He has a wealth of experience which comes after 11 years of international rugby and 79 caps. In this World Cup he did all the basic things which you expect a top-class centre to do. He never missed a tackle or dropped the ball or gave a bad pass. His tackling and covering made him look at times like an extra flanker. His passing was all precision and timing and he orchestrated the whole back division to create opportunities for full back Matt Burke to join the line and make half overlaps and a bit of space for dynamic wings Ben Tune and Joe Roff. If defensive lines had to be cleared, Horan took charge and with either foot was capable of relieving the siege. He was a calming influence on his team-mates, who knew they could rely on him 100 per cent in every situation.

And if all that was not enough, he was also the most incisive and creative centre in the tournament. He has a gloriously wicked little sidestep which momentarily just checks the opposition, then he accelerates through the half gap with an explosive blend of power and pace. Even if he

Wallaby centre and Player of the Tournament Tim Horan leaves French prop Franck Tournaire trailing in his wake as he sets off on a characteristice break at Cardiff.

Though held here by Romeo Gontineac, Horan announced himself by scoring after only two minutes of Australia's opening pool game against Romania in Belfast.

fantastic five weeks. He was tremendous in the line out and dynamite in the open with the ball in his hands. He made big dents against New Zealand in the semi-finals and against Australia in the final and, of course, he scattered lesser opposition in the pool matches to the wind. If he was not the best player in the tournament he was at least the best forward.

Before the semi-finals a lot of people would have put three of the All Blacks' back division on any shortlist, but by the end of the third-place play-off Jonah Lomu, Jeff Wilson and Andrew Mehrtens had all taken a big step backwards. That meant that when the whistle went at the Millennium Stadium to signal that Australia had become the first country to win the World Cup twice, there was no doubt in my mind that their key player and the best player in the tournament was Tim Horan.

Tim Horan enjoys the feeling of lifting the William Webb Ellis Trophy for the second time. He was also a part of Australia's victory at Twickenham in 1991.

does not always break clean through, he bursts across the gain line, and you can immediately hear the opposition alarm bells ringing loud and clear.

Horan has a natural instinct for always doing the right thing, and he has a real insight into the game. He has great vision and looks so good because he seems more often than not to be a split second ahead of the rest in thought and deed. Horan produced all sorts of delicate touches in midfield which made him stand out. In the final he was twice about to receive man and ball, but on each occasion he just flicked the ball on – with one hand once and both hands the second time; he did not risk catching the ball, as he would have been buried in the process. Only players of real class can perform those feats at the highest level. He acted as a catalyst in the knockout stages, doing his own job brilliantly and at the same time making sure he helped to bring out the very best in those around him.

The decision to choose Tim Horan turned out to be very straightforward. The nearest challenger in my mind was probably Abdelatif Benazzi, who had a wonderful tournament for France. It cannot be easy to dominate the World Cup playing in the second row, but Benazzi had a

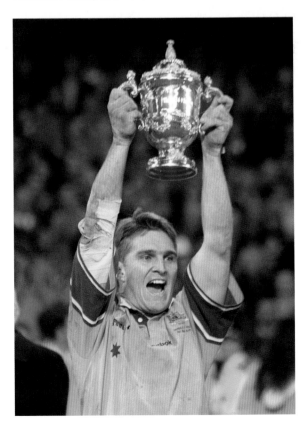

TEAM OF THE TOURNAMENT: AUSTRALIA

Chris Jones

The beer starts to flow in the Wallaby dressing room at the Millennium Stadium after the Australians become the first team to win the Rugby World Cup twice.

I f Rugby World Cup 1999 had a signature team, then it was Australia, the champions. This was a tournament that rewarded ruthless defensive efficiency, and it was fitting that the best team emerged victorious. Yes, the primacy of defence is a sad indictment on the game and its current laws, and David Campese, one of the Wallaby winners in 1991, was left bemoaning the lack of tries and real excitement. For Campo the best game was the France v New Zealand semi-final, and nothing else came close because running rugby took second place to huge defence, then came goal-kicking.

The Australian defence won the World Cup, and it didn't come about by accident. The Wallabies' organisation on the field was the result of two years' hard work and involved so many more players and coaches than outsiders realise. The XV who took the pitch on 6 November at Cardiff will go down in rugby history as the men who

won the cup, but it took a monumental amount of work from the entire squad and the coaching team to establish the pattern of defence which only Juan Grobler, of the USA, managed to beat. His try was the only five-pointer conceded by the Wallabies, which meant they managed to keep everyone out during the knockout stages, and the list of opponents reads: Wales, South Africa and France – not bad!

With any great defence the key elements are communication and commitment. If you are not talking to each other then you are not defending as a single unit and then it comes to every one of the players – yes, including the front row – being prepared to make a big hit. Tackle counts are digested after every match, and players take

A success based on ruthless defensive efficiency. Here Springbok Robbie Fleck gets the treatment at the hands of Wallabies George Gregan, David Giffin and Toutai Kefu.

huge personal pride out of the statistics when they show a big fat zero in the column headed 'Tackles Missed'.

Realignment throughout the game comes down to communication, and it is the key men like scrum half George Gregan who bark out the orders. From his position behind the ruck or maul, he counts the potential attackers and assigns areas of defence to his team-mates. A critical part of the Wallabies' defensive structure is the ability to slow down the opposition ball, and no one does it better than David Wilson, the vastly experienced open-side flanker. Against Wales he was more often a member of the opposition back row than of his own, and this highly competitive individual annoys the hell out of the other team. In the final, French anger boiled over into outright thuggery, with Wilson kicked in the face and left dazed and unable to continue. It was an incident waiting to happen because of the way he plays the game, and cynical former players no doubt felt it was only a question of time before Wilson 'copped a bit'.

The Wallaby game plan starts up front, and while their front row is not going to destroy opponents it stands firm against the best and puts in its share of tackles. In the second row, captain John Eales and David Giffin epitomise the current requirements for players in their positions. They lock the scrum efficiently, provide secure line-out ball using multiple variations and then charge around the pitch clearing out rucks and mauls. After all of that, they are on hand to support the ball carrier or put in big tackles. Who said lock was a position for donkeys?

Backing up the front five are three players of contrasting styles. We have already mentioned Wilson and his ability to slow down ball; he also provides a vital link at the breakdown to maintain continuity. The real grafting work is shared by two players, Matt Cockbain and Owen Finegan. Cockbain is a tall rangy individual who has a great motor, and the Wallabies ask him to run himself into the ground for 60 minutes, and then on comes the even more combative Finegan. Finegan had the glory of scoring a try in the final and is a real dog of a forward; the Wallabies have found a way of using both players' talents to the benefit of the whole team.

One man they did not want to replace at any time in the World Cup was Toutai Kefu. However, he was lost to the team following a ban for punching against Ireland and then signalled his return by proving he was the best ball-carrying forward in the tournament. Kefu has the priceless ability to break through the first tackle and battles hard to stay on his feet, something other big forwards consistently fail to do. When he goes to ground, the ball is invariably won rapidly by the rest of the Wallaby pack that just funnels in behind the big man; in this way, critical momentum is generated for the backs.

Masterminding the attacking plays is Gregan, a livewire scrum half with good vision and the ability to deliver a 'behind the back' reverse pass, which so often catches defences off guard. His quick service allows Stephen Larkham time to use the boot, and this is vital because he is a converted full back with a suspect kicking game. Larkham needs time to transfer the ball to those long legs, and he was charged down on a number of occasions during the tournament. It was a credit to the young man that he kept his confidence up, even though the kicking strategy that underpinned the Wallaby game plan was not natural to him.

Any problems Larkham had were often covered up by the brilliance of Player of the Tournament Tim Horan, whose ability to cut through every opposition back line defied belief. Opponents knew where he would be trying to punch a hole, and still they couldn't stop him. This was epitomised in the final when Abdel Benazzi, the forward of the competition, tried to tackle Horan. In an instant the centre was in and out of contact and ten metres downfield.

Daniel Herbert's big hitting complemented Horan's play, and when this pair did slice through, the outstanding back three of Joe Roff, Ben Tune and goal-kicking Matt Burke provided the pace and power to finish off the move. With the game now back to a tactical kicking pattern it is vital to have a secure back three that can not only field the high kicks but also possess the ability to run the ball back rather than just hoof it downfield. They don't come any better than the Wallaby trio, and, fittingly, they complete the best team of the tournament – a credit to coach Rod Macqueen and all those hours on the training paddock.

With team-mates David Wilson and Richard Harry in attendance, ace goal-kicker and full back Matt Burke launches his injury-time penalty against South Africa.

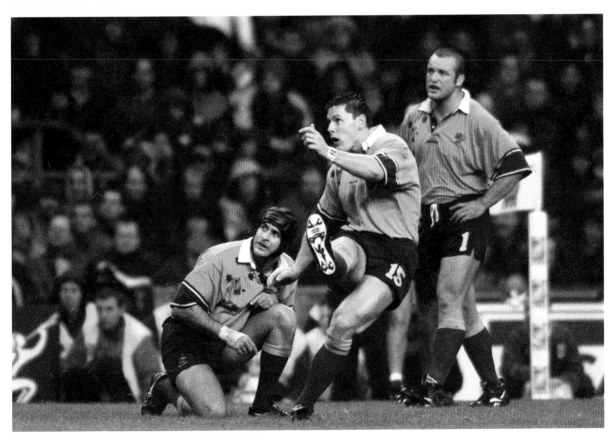

Perhaps you're comfortable with financial information that's almost as precise as a Reuters report.

In which case, run with it.

For us, there's only one kind of information. Information that's based on truth. Truth that's based on integrity. Integrity that's based on impartiality. Impartiality that's based on fact-finding. Fact-finding that's based on self-preservation. Self-preservation? You bet. Our reputation depends on every report we file. Something you won't be slow to grasp.

THE TRUTH. DEAL WITH IT.

REUTERS

RUGBY WORLD CUP 1999
REUTERS DREAM TEAM

Rob Andrew & Willie John McBride

THE BACKS – selected by Rob Andrew

I thought that three full backs stood out in the tournament, with Jeff Wilson and Matt Burke ahead of Shane Howarth mainly beause the Welsh full back dropped out at the quarter-final stage and the other two each played six matches. Wilson was outstanding early on, but he fell from grace in the semi-final against France and did not make up the ground in the third-place play-off match. Matt Burke was a model of consistency all through the tournament and he was not only rock solid in defence, he was tremendous joining the attack to make half overlaps for his wings. Burke gets the vote.

The choice of wings was pretty straightforward. Tana Umaga played well until he had a disappointing match against France, whilst Philippe Bernat-Salles had two good games in the knockout stages. Joe Roff and Christophe Dominici played well all the way through without quite scaling the heights. On the right wing I have selected Ben Tune, who looks a complete player. He has blistering acceleration and plenty of power and is also an elusive runner and a great tackler. On the left wing I go with the top try scorer of the World Cup – Jonah Lomu.

The centre combination was not very difficult. Tim Horan was unquestionably the best back in the World Cup and his name was the first I put down on the team sheet. The choice of his partner lay between his Australian colleague Daniel Herbert and the All Black Christian Cullen. The problem here is that Herbert and Cullen are different types of players. Herbert is a powerhouse; Cullen more of a rapier thrust. Herbert is a great defensive player and support player, whilst Cullen can rip a defence to shreds. But I don't think Cullen did himself full justice in this World Cup. He often looked good in broken play, but I believe he is really a full back or a wing, and he did not look completely at ease in the centre. I have decided to pick Herbert alongside Horan. They were certainly the best team partnership in the tournament.

The choice at half back proved to be the most difficult. In my view there were three excellent scrum halves in Joost van der Westhuizen of South Africa, George Gregan

A little help in the selection process for Willie John McBride from Bill McLaren, Cliff Morgan, Gareth Edwards and biker Ian Robertson (about to shoot off to discuss the backs with Rob Andrew).

of Australia and Agustin Pichot of Argentina. There were also three very good fly halves in Christophe Lamaison of France, Andrew Mehrtens of New Zealand and Stephen Larkham of Australia.

The hardest choice was at scrum half because each of my three nominations enjoyed great success during the tournament. Pichot was the star of the Argentinian team and he left the impression that if he had been playing with one of the big teams he might well have been the star of the World Cup. Unfortunately for him it would be wrong to place too much emphasis on his performance against Japan and Samoa, but it was impossible not to admire his efforts against Wales, Ireland and France.

Gregan was in peak form throughout, but I have decided that van der Westhuizen offers that little bit more and he deserves to be in the Dream Team. He is quick and strong on the break, has a good service, kicks really well, he's an aggressive defender, and, above all, he reads the game superbly.

At fly half, a case could be made for all three of my nominations. Lamaison was a steady influence on the French team, especially in the later stages, but he was not able to create gaps and make breaks so he fills third position. Just ahead of him I have gone for Stephen Larkham, who was a vitally important link in the Wallaby side. However, my choice is Mehrtens because he offers an extra gear in attack and is just as good as the others in every other department of the game.

This back division should be capable of providing a claustrophobic watertight defence and should also be equipped to score a barrowload of tries, containing as it does so many of the best attacking players in world rugby.

On the bench? Fijian lock Emori Katalau storms through the Namibian defence in the opening Pool C match. Katalau was also outstanding against France and England.

THE PACK – selected by Willie John McBride

One of the difficulties in choosing the best composite pack from the World Cup is how to justify the inclusion of one or two really outstanding forwards from countries who made their exit after the pool stage or the quarter-final play-offs. Players like Emori Katalau, the Fijian lock, was absolutely magnificent at the line out and in the loose. He looked the part against France and England, but would he have survived against the All Blacks or Wallabies? Similarly, props Peter Rogers of Wales and Tom Smith of Scotland played really well but made their exit in the quarter-finals. In choosing the best eight forwards I have concentrated on the sides who reached the semi-finals,

and I didn't think any player from any of the other countries would feel hard done by.

A solid scrum gives a team a solid platform, and I have selected the two South African props Os du Randt and Cobus Visagie. Both had excellent World Cups, and I am confident they would lock the Dream Team scrummage and also ensure our line-out jumpers had every possible assistance and protection. Apart from Rogers and Smith, I also considered Richard Harry of Australia at loose-head and Franck Tournaire, Phil Vickery and Andrew Blades at tight-head prop.

My vote for hooker goes to Michael Foley of Australia. He did his job in the scrums, threw in consistently well at the line out and was lively in the loose, both in attack and defence. Keith Wood scored four tries in the match against America, but it was only against America and a hooker's main job is not necessarily scoring tries. Ireland's early exit did not help Wood's cause. Raphael Ibañez captained France well and played well, but he was not as commanding a figure as Foley.

At lock I have chosen Abdelatif Benazzi as the front jumper and John Eales as the middle jumper. I know Martin Johnson of England, David Giffin of Australia and especially Mark Andrews of South Africa all dominated the line out, but I believe the combination of Benazzi and Eales cannot be bettered. I am a real admirer of Mark Andrews, because apart from his expertise at the line out and his mobility and footballing skills in the open he is also a grafter. But John Eales is all those things too, and a top-class captain as well as being a goal-kicker.

At No. 8, I have gone for Toutai Kefu. He is a real impact player with explosive power and pace who was very important to the Australian game plan. I have to say the All Black captain Taine Randell and the Springbok Bobby Skinstad both failed to measure up to the highest standards. At blind-side flanker I have gone for André Venter. The Springboks played left and right flankers, so Venter was not used as an out-and-out blind-side, but I am sure that would be his best position and he had a very good tournament. He is a good footballer, but most important of all he is a real workhorse and fierce tackler.

At open-side I have gone for Olivier Magne, who doesn't shirk any of the game's less glamorous duties – he tackles, covers, rucks and mauls with the best of them – but who is outstanding with the ball in his hands on the attack in the open. I reckon these eight forwards would give our backs every opportunity to display their skills.

Rugby World Cup 1999
Reuters Dream Team

 14

B. Tune

15

M. Burke

 11

J. Lomu

13

D. Herbert

12

T. Horan

10

A. Mehrtens

9

J. vd Westhuizen

 1

O. du Randt

2

M. Foley

3

C. Visagie

4

A. Benazzi

5

J. Eales (c)

 6

A. Venter

8

T. Kefu

7

O. Magne

THE GREATEST DISAPPOINTMENT: ENGLAND

Chris Jones

Clive Woodward and Mike Catt watch England go down against the All Blacks. Are England to be limited to one-off successes against the southern hemisphere?

Claude Skrela's unpredictable French who became the standard-bearers for the top half of the planet. Woodward and his England men were reduced to the role of interested spectators, and this fall from rugby grace was only too blindingly obvious to men like Lawrence Dallaglio, the ex-captain, who had to lead his London Wasps team against Newcastle in an Allied Dunbar Premiership First Division game at Loftus Road in front of less than 3000 as the tasteless meat in the middle of a World Cup semi-final sandwich. That game took place on the Saturday evening after Australia had recorded a heart-stopping extra-time win over holders South Africa, and 12 hours later the sport enjoyed one of those unforgettable moments, when the French destroyed New Zealand's cup dreams at Twickenham.

Those two semi-finals only served to highlight the size of the missed opportunity England had thrown away with their pallid performance against the Springboks in Paris. In 1991, a pragmatic England team had reached the final, and a nation rejoiced with a rugby fervour never witnessed before. Mini-rugby sections at clubs all over the country reported phenomenal increases in attendances, and the feel-good factor generated by England's run to the final – where they lost to Australia – raised the game to new heights of public recognition.

Eight years on and the feeling was 'Is that it?' England had flattered to deceive, and the post-Paris analysis centred around Woodward's credentials as an international coach – 14 wins, 12 defeats and two draws. It's a record of constant failure to beat the southern hemisphere giants and raises the real possibility that England can only ever hope to register the occasional one-off triumph because their playing structure just doesn't prepare the players for that kind of sustained challenge.

Woodward's tinkering with selection and a constant battle to get key men fit must be taken into consideration, along with the club-based playing programme, but almost

W hat can you buy for £8 million? If you are Clive Woodward, the England coach, the answer is a rather disappointing quarter-final place at the greatest rugby show on earth. That enormous sum of money is the estimated cost of England's World Cup campaign, and you don't have to be the Chancellor of the Exchequer to work out that the return on that particular investment was poor.

England were supposed to carry the hopes of the northern hemisphere nations into at least the semi-finals against the Tri-Nations giants of South Africa, New Zealand and Australia, but it turned out to be Jean-

everything else was put in place for England to mount a credible World Cup campaign. No other England squad had ever been given a blank cheque and told to win the cup. Woodward got everything he wanted, from a month-long training camp in Australia to gruelling sessions with the Royal Marines at Lympstone. Every player received a lap-top computer so that Woodward could e-mail out his thoughts and instructions, and it appeared that England, the great dinosaur of world rugby, was finally embracing the twenty-first century.

It had always been a mystery to every other major rugby nation that England, with more clubs and players than anyone else, had never won the World Cup. Many of those countries failed to notice that English rugby was based on a club system, not on state or provincial teams, and as the new century arrives this fundamental problem remains at the heart of the raging debate. Fran Cotton, chairman of Club England, is the man who has banged on longer than most for another level of competition for his English players, one that can go some way to mirroring the Super-12 tournament that has been so important Down Under.

Thanks to England's decision to treat the arrival of professionalism in 1995 as a problem that may go away if you ignored it for 12 months, the leading players were contracted to their clubs and not by the Union. England imposed a moratorium during that 12 months which, in effect, meant they did nothing while the rest of the game embraced professionalism. When the Rugby Football Union finally decided to get its hands grubby and pick up the professional ball, they found the players belonged to the clubs. Staggeringly, the governing body now had to go cap in hand to its member clubs to ask if they would mind releasing the players for the odd international!

The two sides are now closer, but Cotton and Woodward still want to have the top players under an RFU contract to ensure total control over the playing and training regimes of the country's elite. To South African, Australian and New Zealand rugby chiefs this is an unbelievable situation. They just cannot understand how a system can exist where the national coach does not dictate when and where the top players play. Woodward, if he decides he still wants to battle on against the odds, can only hope that Cotton wins the day and substantial change is instigated to give his players a new level of rugby.

England's quarter-final exit proved that the current squad contains players unable to make critical decisions under pressure because they do not face that kind of constant problem away from the international arena. The introduction of a British or European league could go some way to bridging the gap between club and Test levels, but it will require the agreement of five separate unions to bring about fundamental change. England fans have suffered too many years of wasteful infighting already, and the thought of another round of bickering and back-stabbing leaves everyone cold. Almost as cold as they felt in the minutes after England had traipsed off the Stade de France pitch, consigned to the role of also-rans in Rugby World Cup 1999. What a poor return for all that hard work and money.

A gutted Martin Johnson leaves the field after England's semi-final defeat by South Africa. Can England succeed at international level under their current domestic system?

Interviews

Captain Fantastic

John Eales

Congratulations, John. How does it feel to be the first person to lift the Webb Ellis Trophy twice?

Obviously we are very proud that the team has been able to go out and win in Cardiff and that we've been part of our own piece of history. From our point of view it's been a long time, four years probably, that we've been talking about it – much more specifically over the last two years. If I can say from everyone in the team's point of view there's been a lot of sacrifices made along the way, not only by the XV but by the whole squad – we've got a touring party over here of 40, or a couple more – and also everyone back home. The sacrifices they've made to give us the opportunity to be here today makes it even more special.

John Eales in World Cup action. Winning required 'a lot of sacrifices made along the way, not only by the XV but by the whole squad...and also everyone back home.'

Looking at the final itself, did the French team perform as you expected or were you surprised at the ease of your victory?

All week, right from the time we saw the way the French played against the All Blacks, we knew how tough the game was going to be, and we certainly weren't let down out there. The side was very nervous right through the week leading up to the game, very concerned about the way the French play because they are so dangerous from anywhere on the field. We did a lot of homework on them and we weren't disappointed at all with the way they played. They came out very strongly and they kept going throughout the match. They played some great rugby.

Once again the Australian defence kept a clean sheet. In fact you only conceded one try in the whole tournament. How much emphasis did you put on defence?

We took a lot of pride in our defence; we always do. It was something we spoke about at various stages, not just during the game but before it as well. It's been a feature of Australian teams of the past, and it's been a feature of all teams that have won the World Cup before, so we knew it was going to be important.

At half-time Australia were still only 12-6 ahead. You gathered the team round you. What did you say to them?

We just spoke about what we wanted to do in the second half. Basically we thought we had gone pretty well in the first half and hadn't capitalised on the opportunities that we had created and we had a lot of confidence that if we kept going, if we put the pressure on, then the points would come. That's basically all that was said. Then we went out there and did the job.

Given your known Republican sentiments, can you tell us what was said between you and the Queen when she handed you the cup?

I can't remember exactly. I think I just said, 'Thanks very much, your Majesty…it's a very special moment'; something like that.

Almost there! John Eales raises his arms in triumph as replacement flanker Owen Finegan touches down for Australia's second try in the 86th minute of the final.

And when you and your team put the trophy on the ground and formed a circle around it, what was that all about?

We just got out there, put the cup in the middle and sang our national anthem. One of the good things about the team is the pride we have in being Australian. That was just a celebration for us and also for all the supporters who were there today and for all the supporters back home. Hopefully they got a feel of that too.

How do you compare this achievement with 1991?

Well, they were both very special, for different reasons, and for a lot of the same reasons. In both cases we had teams that were very enthusiastic and had a very strong will to win, had very strong goals and were able to achieve those goals. Probably in the aftermath of both occasions today was a little bit better because we were able to run around the field and actually thank our fans who were in the ground, whereas in 1991 everyone invaded the pitch straightaway. It was great for the team to have those moments after the game.

PLANNING MAKES PERFECT
ROD MACQUEEN

Coach to the world champions – this must be a wonderful feeling.

Yes, it's always nice to see rewards going to people who put in so much hard work, and certainly this team has done that. I'm just chuffed to see them celebrating. They can enjoy themselves as much as they like now.

When did you start to believe that you could win the title?

Well, obviously that had to be our goal from day one. If you set yourselves goals, you've got to expect to get there. In particular we knew that we had to change if we were to be successful, and that's not just the players and the support staff but also their families. It is a very demanding sport these days and it's nice to see the players reaping the reward of all the effort they have put in. We had planned this all the way through and it was just nice to see something that had been planned for so long come off.

Rod Macqueen with the World Cup flanked by assistant coaches Tim Lane (left) and Jeff Miller. 'It was just nice to see something that had been planned for so long come off.'

What sort of support did you get from people back home in Australia?

We had some wonderful support. Most people know we got a fax from the commander of the forces in East Timor and that was read to the team before the game. On top of that there were faxes from people like the Prime Minister down to, as John Eales put it, the greengrocer in the street. We had faxes from all walks of life in Australia across the board. It was wonderful support and there was no way we were going to go into that game without feeling that we had a lot to fulfil and that we were playing for pride in Australia.

Did everything go as you planned in the final?

Pretty much. I don't think anything works exactly as you

plan it. We went through some tough times against France and in every match, times when you have to work very hard. What I was particularly pleased about was that we always kept overcoming them. I felt we were always in control. France played very well. There were a few indiscretions that our players were able to get over. We suffered a number of gouged eyes, and the unfortunate thing is that France don't need to do that because they are a good team. But I was happy our guys were able to overcome that. They went into the game knowing they would have to play well to win it and I'm really pleased they did.

There have been outstanding performances from so many of them. Who were the key performers for Australia?

You can't pick anyone out. The thing I'm most pleased about is that it was a great team effort. They've stuck together. We haven't had to rely on any one individual. Right across the board there haven't been any weaknesses and I think that's what we've been striving to do.

Have there been times when the doubts sneaked in?

There are always times when doubts sneak in. You wouldn't be human if that wasn't the case. We've had our ups and downs over the last two years. We've trodden a fine line here and there but generally we've been on focus. But for 42 people to come away for nine weeks and to have the sort of harmony we've had is a credit to the team,

and the way they have stuck together and the sacrifices they have made has been incredible. They might not have agreed with a lot of things but they put the team first and I'm very happy with them.

It's really been striking this wonderful atmosphere amongst the players. Even at training for example they all seem to get on so well.

They've got a wonderful sense of humour. They are a great bunch of guys and I just think they've got what they deserve.

How big a role did captain John Eales play?

Huge. It was great for Australia that he came back from injury when he did – as it's turned out both him and Stephen Larkham being involved has been really good for us. John's captaincy has definitely helped us a lot and he can be proud of himself. I believe he's now Australia's most capped captain and we're very happy to have him – hopefully for at least a couple more years. I think all the people out in Australia can be very proud of him and the way he represents his country, and the ambassador he is.

So what's next for Australia and Rod Macqueen?

It's far too early to talk about that. I'm just looking forward to seeing my wife!

The Australian Rugby World Cup 1999 squad. 'For 42 people to come away for nine weeks and to have the sort of harmony we've had is a credit to the team.'

SAME AGAIN – ONLY BETTER
TIM HORAN

An obvious question to start with – how does it feel to have won the World Cup twice?

Fantastic. It did take some time to sink in. In fact it was 45 minutes after the final whistle before it really hit me that we were world champions. We've had some fantastic support from all the fans back home and with all the faxes and well-wishers it's really been a country effort.

Once again you personally had a great tournament, and another fantastic performance in the final. You must be more than pleased with your form.

I was very pleased. For a rugby player, I'm getting on a bit so I was very happy with the way I played. You know my thoughts on winning the first World Cup were that that would be plenty for me, but a second World Cup is unbelievable. You know, it's not a dream come true

Tim Horan in action against South Africa. 'My thoughts on winning the first World Cup were that that would be plenty for me, but a second World Cup is unbelievable.'

because I never dreamt that I would win two World Cups. It's hard to believe, but it's even better for all the guys who haven't won a World Cup before, and a lot of guys can say they've got their hands on the World Cup, they're world champions now. For every one of them and all our support staff, it's a fantastic achievement that has been building over the last two years.

And fantastic too for your old centre partner Jason Little. He was on there at outside centre, you at inside, for most of the second half. That must have brought back the memories.

Yeah, it was great to be back together. A shame for Daniel Herbert that he had to go off with knee ligament trouble, but great to renew our partnership. Jason's been around a long time and we've been through a lot together, so it was fantastic that we could enjoy this experience as well. The forwards had done such a good job getting us across the advantage line, that we were always in control. The support was always there so it made our job so much easier.

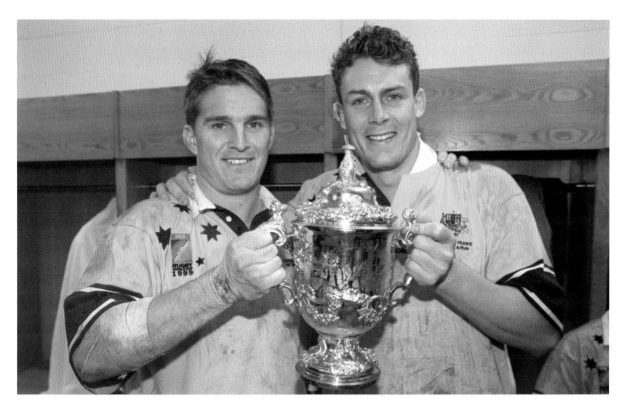

As you say, Australia were always in control, but it was only, I suppose, when Owen Finegan scored that late try that you could relax.

Yeah, I couldn't believe it could happen like that. The only similar try I can remember was scored by a Canberra Rugby League player in the Grand Final in extra time about eight years ago! It was great to see a forward score. We knew we would have a lot more pressure on us out in the back because of the way we had gone in the South Africa game, so we knew we had to try a few moves amongst the forwards, off the back of line outs. It was just great when they came off.

So, when you were presented your medal by the Queen, what did it mean to you?

It was fantastic. There are some great moments in your life – when you get married, when your children are born, and this was right up there with them. It was unbelievable, a great thrill. I shall treasure it for ever, and when I look back on my rugby career I can go to my grave reasonably happy in the knowledge that I have helped to win two World Cups.

But what about a third? You're still young enough. What about playing in Australia in 2003?

Horan celebrates World Cup success with Jason Little, also his centre partner when Australia won the cup in 1991. At Cardiff, Little came on for the injured Daniel Herbert.

No, I won't be around by then. But I can say I've thoroughly enjoyed this tour. This is a very happy team. They've been very jovial, as you've probably seen But they know when to switch on and when to switch off. They go training and obviously everyone's very serious, but after that we've been a fairly light-hearted side.

Do you think that was the key – that you got on so well together?

I think so for sure. when we first came across to Ireland at the beginning of the tournament, we were able to play golf, forget about training and just bond together. That really helped. We were confident of our fitness and we always timed the build-up so we weren't always fired up to play the game two days ahead of the match itself. Coming to the final itself, we were nervous, but so were they. But we knew that we had to play to our strengths, in defence, in the forwards, and put pressure on them, get them to make the mistakes and create the position from which Matt Burke could kick the goals. It worked.

RENAISSANCE – AND DISAPPOINTMENT RAPHAEL IBAÑEZ

A second World Cup final for France, a second disappointment. Yet you must be proud of your team's efforts in the tournament.

Yes, I am very, very proud. This World Cup has been a great adventure for us, but in the end we lost to a very good team. They have some very good individual players, but the best thing is the way they played for each other. They were very well organised and deserved to win.

Where did it go wrong for France?

There was too much indiscipline and too many errors from the French team. Then as the score mounted up they started playing for themselves and not for the team.

How much had that marvellous semi-final win over the All Blacks taken out of the players?

Quite a lot. I think that the players were not quite as focused as we were a week ago, against the All Blacks. We were a lot more nervous and, strangely enough, a lot less confident. I spent the week, as I had done before the All Black match, drummimg it into the players that we could win, but sadly on the day we couldn't repeat the same sort of performance.

That game against New Zealand has been described as perhaps the greatest World Cup match ever. Was there a sense that you had already made history before going out to face Australia?

Actually, I was surprised to hear the game described as one of the best ever. It was a very physical game, a very good game with plenty of movement and plenty of tries. In a sense it was our final, although we didn't think so at the time.

But you must have been aware of the write-ups of that game and especially the extraordinary outpouring of emotion about it in France.

Well, I did receive a telephone call in the dressing room from the President of France! But we had to travel from Twickenham to Cardiff and concentrate on our next game

so I don't think we fully understood what it meant to people in France. Sure, our families told us how happy they were for us, but the main thing for us was to forget the fuss and concentrate on beating the Wallabies.

How much were you aware that you were carrying the hopes of the whole of northern hemisphere rugby?

Once it became obvious that we were the only northern hemisphere side left in the semi-finals, we hoped that the people of Europe would get behind us. I think it is important for the game in Europe to have a European team in the final. I said before we played New Zealand that I hoped that the Twickenham crowd would support us but I didn't expect it. They were fantastic then and also in Cardiff. I was sorry to disappoint them.

But looking back on France's World Cup, you must be reasonably happy?

Yes, for the team and for myself. You know, this year has been difficult for me. After the Grand Slam we have had a number of defeats, which have been hard to live with. As the captain, I was criticised a lot, which is logical. So to have some success has for me been a little revenge.

Has France now got the right blend of players and styles?

Yes, I think so. People are always talking about French flair. But you must have the other things as well – the ability to make tackles, to kick well, to be organised in defence and attack. That is what the Wallabies had. They deserved to be world champions, but my country and the rest of Europe can be proud of France.

Raphael Ibañez, the French hooker and captain, celebrates a French try during his side's extraordinary semi-final victory over New Zealand.

When it comes to sports results, you could say we really know the score.

In sports - just like business - results are everything. And not just to the millions worldwide who depend on our systems to deliver real-time scores and analysis of premier sporting events on the Web and on TV - but to the networks and press that cover them. Events like the Volvo PGA Championship, the Trophée Lancôme, the Volvo Scandinavian Masters and others on the PGA European Tour, the Open Championship, the US Open, U.S. Seniors Open, U.S. Women's Open, Australian Open, Rugby World Cup, Macau Grand Prix and many more. We ensure the results keep pouring in thanks to the powerful teaming of Unisys software, Windows NT servers and our dedicated people. It's the same combination our customers around the world rely on to solve their real-time business problems and get them results. Which is why we take sports very seriously - it's what keeps us ahead of the game. www.unisys.com.

UNISYS

We eat, sleep and drink this stuff.

Statistics

UNISYS in association with HOURGLASS VISION

Rugby World Cup 1987-1999

Highest scores:
145   New Zealand v Japan (Bloemfontein, 1995)
101   New Zealand v Italy (Huddersfield, 1999)
101   England v Tonga (Twickenham, 1999)

Biggest winning margin:
128   New Zealand v Japan (Bloemfontein, 1995)
98   New Zealand v Italy (Huddersfield, 1999)
91   England v Tonga (Twickenham, 1999)

Most points by a player in a match:
45   Simon Culhane (New Zealand v Japan, 1995)
44   Gavin Hastings (Scotland v Ivory Coast, 1995)
47   Paul Grayson (England v Tonga, 1999)

Most tries by a player in a match:
6   Marc Ellis (New Zealand v Japan, 1995)
4   Ieuan Evans (Wales v Canada, 1987)
    John Gallagher (New Zealand v Fiji, 1987)
    Craig Green (New Zealand v Fiji, 1987)
    Gavin Hastings (Scotland v Ivory Coast, 1995)
    Jonah Lomu (New Zealand v England, 1995)
    Brian Robinson (Ireland v Zimbabwe, 1991)
    Chester Williams (South Africa v W. Samoa, 1995)
    Keith Wood (Ireland v United States, 1999)

Most points in one tournament:
126   Grant Fox (New Zealand, 1987)
112   Thierry Lacroix (France, 1995)
104   Gavin Hastings (Scotland, 1995)

Leading aggregate World Cup scorers:
227   Gavin Hastings (Scotland, 1987, 1991, 1995)
195   Michael Lynagh (Australia, 1987, 1991, 1995)
170   Grant Fox (New Zealand, 1987, 1991)

Most tries in World Cups:
15   Jonah Lomu (New Zealand, 1995, 1999)
11   Rory Underwood (England, 1987, 1991, 1995)
10   David Campese (Australia, 1987, 1991, 1995)

Most tries in one tournament:
8   Jonah Lomu (New Zealand, 1999)
7   Marc Ellis (New Zealand, 1995)
    Jonah Lomu (New Zealand, 1995)

Most tries in a match by a team:
21   New Zealand v Japan (Bloemfontein, 1995)

Most penalty goals in World Cups:
33   Andrew Mehrtens (New Zealand, 1995, 1999)
31   Gonzalo Quesada (Argentina, 1999)
31   Michael Lynagh (Australia, 1991, 1995)

Most penalty goals in one tournament:
31   Gonzalo Quesada (Argentina, 1999)
26   Thierry Lacroix (France, 1995)
21   Grant Fox (New Zealand, 1987)

Most conversions in World Cups:
39   Gavin Hastings (Scotland, 1987, 1991, 1995)
37   Grant Fox (New Zealand, 1987, 1991)
36   Michael Lynagh (Australia, 1987, 1991, 1995)

Most conversions in one tournament:
30   Grant Fox (New Zealand, 1987)
20   Michael Lynagh (Australia, 1987)
    Simon Culhane (New Zealand, 1995)

Most dropped goals in World Cups:
6   Jannie de Beer (South Africa, 1999)
5   Rob Andrew (England, 1987, 1991, 1995)

Most dropped goals in one tournament:
6   Jannie de Beer (South Africa, 1999)
3   Rob Andrew (England, 1995)
    Andrew Mehrtens (New Zealand, 1995)
    Joel Stransky (South Africa, 1995)
    Gregor Townsend (Scotland, 1999)

Most dropped goals in one match by a team:
5   South Africa v England (Paris, 1999)
3   Fiji v Romania (Brive, 1991)

Rugby World Cup 1999

Leading point scorers

Player	Team	Points	T	C	P	DG
Gonzalo Quesada	Argentina	102	0	3	31	1
Matthew Burke	Australia	101	2	17	19	0
Jannie de Beer	South Africa	97	0	17	15	6
Andrew Mehrtens	New Zealand	79	0	11	19	0
Jonny Wilkinson	England	69	1	8	16	0
Christophe Lamaison	France	65	1	9	12	2
Silao Leaega	Samoa	62	2	11	10	0
Neil Jenkins	Wales	57	0	12	11	0
Paul Grayson	England	54	0	12	10	0
Kenny Logan	Scotland	51	0	9	11	0
Gareth Rees	Canada	49	0	11	8	1
Richard Dourthe	France	45	1	8	8	0
David Humphreys	Ireland	41	0	4	10	1
Jonah Lomu	New Zealand	40	8	0	0	0
Waisale Serevi	Fiji	39	0	9	7	0
Tony Brown	New Zealand	36	1	11	3	0
Diego Dominguez	Italy	30	1	2	7	0
Jeff Wilson	New Zealand	30	6	0	0	0
Kevin Dalzell	United States	29	1	3	6	0
Keiji Hirose	Japan	26	0	1	8	0
Petre Mitu	Romania	25	0	2	7	0
Nicky Little	Fiji	24	0	6	3	1
Sateki Tu'ipulotu	Tonga	23	1	3	3	1
Leandre Van Dyk	Namibia	22	0	2	6	0
Philippe Bernat-Salles	France	20	4	0	0	0
Eric Elwood	Ireland	20	0	7	2	0
Dan Luger	England	20	4	0	0	0
Viliame Satala	Fiji	20	4	0	0	0
Keith Wood	Ireland	20	4	0	0	0

Most tries

Player	Team	Tries
Jonah Lomu	New Zealand	8
Jeff Wilson	New Zealand	6
Philippe Bernat-Salles	France	4
Dan Luger	England	4
Viliame Satala	Fiji	4
Keith Wood	Ireland	4
Phil Greening	England	3
Toutai Kefu	Australia	3
Martin Leslie	Scotland	3
Brian Lima	Samoa	3
Ugo Mola	France	3
Cameron Murray	Scotland	3
Emile Ntamack	France	3
Mark Taylor	Wales	3
Ben Tune	Australia	3
Joost vd Westhuizen	South Africa	3
Morgan Williams	Canada	3

Most penalty goals

Player	Team	Penalties
Gonzalo Quesada	Argentina	31
Matthew Burke	Australia	19
Andrew Mehrtens	New Zealand	19
Jonny Wilkinson	England	16
Jannie de Beer	South Africa	15
Christophe Lamaison	France	12
Neil Jenkins	Wales	11
Kenny Logan	Scotland	11
Silao Leaega	Samoa	10
Paul Grayson	England	10
David Humphreys	Ireland	10

Most conversions

Player	Team	Conversions
Matthew Burke	Australia	17
Jannie de Beer	South Africa	17
Neil Jenkins	Wales	12
Paul Grayson	England	12
Andrew Mehrtens	New Zealand	11
Silao Leaega	Samoa	11
Gareth Rees	Canada	11
Tony Brown	New Zealand	11

Dropped goals

Player	Team	Dropped Goals
Jannie de Beer	South Africa	6
Gregor Townsend	Scotland	3
Christophe Lamaison	France	2
Percy Montgomery	South Africa	2
David Humphreys	Ireland	1
Stephen Larkham	Australia	1
Nicky Little	Fiji	1
David Niu	United States	1
Brian O'Driscoll	Ireland	1
Gonzalo Quesada	Argentina	1
Gareth Rees	Canada	1
Sateki Tu'ipulotu	Tonga	1

Highest kicking success rates

Player	Team	Goals	Attempts	Rate
Felipe Contepomi	Argentina	2	2	100
Gareth Rees	Canada	19	19	100
Diego Aguirre	Uruguay	6	6	100
David Humphreys	Ireland	14	15	93
Eric Elwood	Ireland	9	10	90
Paul Grayson	England	22	25	88
Waisale Serevi	Fiji	16	18	88
Jannie de Beer	South Africa	32	36	88
Christophe Lamaison	France	21	24	87
Andrei Kovalenco	Spain	5	6	83
Gonzalo Quesada	Argentina	34	41	82
Tony Brown	New Zealand	14	17	82
Nicky Little	Fiji	9	11	81
Diego Dominguez	Italy	9	11	81
Keiji Hirose	Japan	9	11	81
Henry Honiball	South Africa	4	5	80
Kenny Logan	Scotland	20	26	76
Neil Jenkins	Wales	23	30	76
Andrew Mehrtens	New Zealand	30	40	75
Silao Leaega	Samoa	21	28	75
Matthew Burke	Australia	36	49	73
Richard Dourthe	France	16	23	69
Petre Mitu	Romania	9	13	69
Jonny Wilkinson	England	24	35	68
John Eales	Australia	2	3	66
Bobby Ross	Canada	2	3	66
Leandre Van Dyk	Namibia	8	12	66
Duncan Hodge	Scotland	6	9	66
Sateki Tu'ipulotu	Tonga	6	9	66

Pool A

Pool B

Galashiels 2.10.99

Spain 15	Uruguay 27
Pens: Kovalenco (5)	Tries: Ormaechea, pen try, Cardoso, Menchaca
	Cons: D Aguirre (2)
	Pens: D Aguirre

	Spain		Uruguay
15	Miguel Angel Frechilla	15	Alfonso Cardoso
14	Oriol Ripol	14	Martin Ferres
13	Alvar Enciso	13	Pedro Vecino
12	Sebastian Loubsens	12	Martin Mendaro
11	Rafael Bastide	11	Pablo Costabile
10	Andrei Kovalenco	10	Diego Aguirre
9	Jaime Alonso	9	Federico Sciarra
1	Jordi Camps	1	Rodrigo Sanchez
2	Fernando de la Calle	2	Diego Lamelas
3	Jose Ignacio Zapatero	3	Pablo Lemoine
4	Jose Miguel Villau	4	Juan Carlos Bado
5	Sergio Souto	5	Mario Lame
6	Jose Diaz	6	Nicolas Brignoni
7	Carlos Souto	7	Martin Panizza
8	Alberto Malo (c)	8	Diego Ormaechea (c)
16	Francisco Puertas	16	Juan Menchaca *
17	Aitor Etxeberria	17	Fernando Sosa Diaz *
18	Aratz Gallastegui	18	Agustin Ponce de Leon *
19	Alfonso Mata	19	Nicolas Grille *
20	Oskar Astarloa *	20	Juan Alzueta
21	Victor Torres	21	Guillermo Storace *
22	Diego Zarzosa *	22	Francisco de los Santos *

Referee: Chris White

Murrayfield 10.10.99

South Africa 47	Spain 3
Tries: Vos (2), Leonard, Muller, pen try, Skinstad, Swanepoel	Pens: Velasco
Cons: De Beer (6)	

	South Africa		Spain
15	Breyton Paulse	15	Francisco Puertas
14	Stefan Terblanche	14	Jose Ignacio Inchausti
13	Wayne Julies	13	Alberto Socias
12	Pieter Muller	12	Fernando Diez
11	Kaya Molotana	11	Miguel Angel Frechilla
10	Jannie de Beer	10	Aitor Etxeberria
9	Werner Swanepoel	9	Aratz Gallastegui
1	Ollie le Roux	1	Jordi Camps
2	Chris Rossouw	2	Diego Zarzosa
3	Adrian Garvey	3	Jose Ignacio Zapatero
4	Fritz van Heerden	4	Jose Miguel Villau
5	Krynauw Otto	5	Oskar Astarloa
6	Ruben Kruger	6	Jose Diaz
7	Anton Leonard	7	Carlos Souto
8	Andre Vos (c)	8	Alberto Malo (c)
16	Deon Kayser	16	Ferran Velasco *
17	Percy Montgomery	17	Antonio Socias
18	Joost vd Westhuizen *	18	Jaime Alonso
19	Bobby Skinstad *	19	Alfonso Mata *
20	Mark Andrews	20	Luis Javier Martinez *
21	Os du Randt *	21	Victor Torres *
22	Naka Drotske	22	Fernando de la Calle *

Referee: Paul Honiss

Twickenham 2.10.99

England 67	Italy 7
Tries: Dawson, Hill, De Glanville, Perry, Wilkinson, Luger, Back, Corry	Tries: Dominguez
Cons: Wilkinson (6)	Cons: Dominguez
Pens: Wilkinson (5)	

	England		Italy
15	Matt Perry	15	Matt Pini
14	Dan Luger	14	Paolo Vaccari
13	Will Greenwood	13	Christian Stoica
12	Phil de Glanville	12	Luca Martin
11	Austin Healey	11	Nicolas Zisti
10	Jonny Wilkinson	10	Diego Dominguez
9	Matt Dawson	9	Alessandro Troncon
1	Jason Leonard	1	Frederico Pucciariello
2	Richard Cockerill	2	Alessandro Moscardi
3	Phil Vickery	3	Franco Properzi-Curti
4	Martin Johnson (c)	4	Valter Cristoletto
5	Danny Grewcock	5	Mark Giacheri
6	Richard Hill	6	Massimo Giovanelli (c)
7	Neil Back	7	Mauro Bergamasco
8	Lawrence Dallaglio	8	Orazio Arancio
16	Nick Beal *	16	Nicola Mazzucato *
17	Jeremy Guscott *	17	Francesco Mazzariol *
18	Paul Grayson *	18	Giampiero Mazzi
19	Martin Corry *	19	Andrea de Rossi *
20	Darren Garforth *	20	Carlo Checchinato *
21	Graham Rowntree *	21	Andrea Castellani
22	Phil Greening *	22	Andrea Moretti

Referee: Andre Watson

Leicester 10.10.99

Italy 25	Tonga 28
Tries: Moscardi	Tries: Taufahema, S Tu'ipulotu, Fatani
Cons: Dominguez	Cons: S Tu'ipulotu (2)
Pens: Dominguez (6)	Pens: S Tu'ipulotu (2)
	DG: S Tu'ipulotu

	Italy		Tonga
15	Matt Pini	15	Sateki Tu'ipulotu
14	Paolo Vaccari	14	Taunaholo Taufahema
13	Christian Stoica	13	Semi Taupeaafe
12	Alessandro Ceppolino	12	'Eli Vunipola (c)
11	Fabio Roselli	11	'Epeli Taione
10	Diego Dominguez	10	Brian Woolley
9	Alessandro Troncon	9	Sililo Martens
1	Alessandro Moreno	1	Ta'u fi'inga'anuku
2	Alessandro Moscardi	2	Latiume Maka
3	Andrea Castellani	3	Ngalu Taufo'ou
4	Carlo Checchinato	4	Falamani Mafi
5	Mark Giacheri	5	Benhur Kivalu
6	Massimo Giovanelli (c)	6	David Edwards
7	Stefano Saviozzi	7	Sonatane Koloi
8	Carlo Caione	8	Katilimoni Tu'ipulotu
16	Nicola Mazzucato *	16	Fifita Puku Faletau
17	Francesco Mazzariol *	17	Tevita Tiueti *
18	Giampiero Mazzi	18	'Isi Tapueluelu *
19	Orazio Arancio	19	Mat Te Pou *
20	Valter Cristofoletto *	20	'Isileli Fatani *
21	Franco Properzi-Curti *	21	Damien Penisini
22	Andrea Moretti *	22	Sione Mone Tu'ipulotu

Referee: David McHugh

Murrayfield 3.10.99

Scotland 29	South Africa 46
Tries: M Leslie, Tait	Tries: B Venter, Fleck, Le Roux, Kayser, A Venter, Van der Westhuizen
Cons: Logan (2)	Cons: De Beer (4), Montgomery
Pens: Logan (4)	Pens: De Beer (2)
DG: Townsend	

	Scotland		South Africa
15	Glenn Metcalfe	15	Percy Montgomery
14	Cameron Murray	14	Deon Kayser
13	Alan Tait	13	Robbie Fleck
12	John Leslie	12	Brendan Venter
11	Kenny Logan	11	Pieter Rossouw
10	Gregor Townsend	10	Jannie de Beer
9	Gary Armstrong (c)	9	Joost vd Westhuizen (c)
1	Tom Smith	1	Os du Randt
2	Gordon Bulloch	2	Naka Drotske
3	George Graham	3	Cobus Visagie
4	Scott Murray	4	Albert van den Berg
5	Stuart Grimes	5	Mark Andrews
6	Martin Leslie	6	Rassie Erasmus
7	Budge Pountney	7	Andre Venter
8	Gordon Simpson	8	Bobby Skinstad
16	Jamie Mayer *	16	Chris Rossouw
17	Duncan Hodge	17	Ollie le Roux *
18	Bryan Redpath	18	Krynauw Otto *
19	Peter Walton *	19	Andre Vos *
20	Doddie Weir *	20	Werner Swanepoel
21	David Hilton *	21	Pieter Muller
22	Robert Russell *	22	Breyton Paulse

Referee: Colin Hawke

Glasgow 15.10.99

South Africa 39	Uruguay 3
Tries: Fleck, Van der Westhuizen, Kayser, Van den Berg	Pens: D Aguirre
Cons: De Beer (4)	
Pens: De Beer (2)	

	South Africa		Uruguay
15	Percy Montgomery	15	Alfonso Cardoso
14	Deon Kayser	14	Juan Menchaca
13	Robbie Fleck	13	Pedro Vecino
12	Brendan Venter	12	Fernando Paullier
11	Pieter Rossouw	11	Pablo Costabile
10	Jannie de Beer	10	Diego Aguirre
9	Joost vd Westhuizen (c)	9	Fernando Sosa Diaz
1	Os du Randt	1	Rodrigo Sanchez
2	Naka Drotske	2	Diego Lamelas
3	Cobus Visagie	3	Pablo Lemoine
4	Krynauw Otto	4	Juan Carlos Bado
5	Mark Andrews	5	Mario Lame
6	Rassie Erasmus	6	Nicolas Grille
7	Andre Venter	7	Martin Panizza
8	Bobby Skinstad	8	Diego Ormaechea (c)
16	Stefan Terblanche	16	Jose Viana *
17	Pieter Muller	17	Sebastian Aguirre *
18	Werner Swanepoel	18	Nicolas Brignoni *
19	Andre Vos	19	Eduardo Berruti *
20	Albert van den Berg *	20	Juan Alzueta *
21	Ollie le Roux *	21	Guillermo Storace *
22	Chris Rossouw	22	Francisco de los Santos

Referee: Peter Marshall

Bristol 3.10.99

New Zealand 45	Tonga 9
Tries: Lomu (2), Kronfeld, Maxwell, Kelleher	Pens: Taumalolo (3)
Cons: Mehrtens (4)	
Pens: Mehrtens (4)	

	New Zealand		Tonga
15	Jeff Wilson	15	Siua Taumalolo
14	Tana Umaga	14	Fepi'kou Tatafu
13	Christian Cullen	13	Tevita Tiueti
12	Alama Ieremia	12	Semi Taupeaafe
11	Jonah Lomu	11	Latiume Maka
10	Andrew Mehrtens	10	'Elisi Vunipola (c)
9	Justin Marshall	9	Sililo Martens
1	Carl Hoeft	1	Ta'u Fa'inga'anuku
2	Anton Oliver	2	Fe'ao Vunipola
3	Kees Meeuws	3	Tevita Taumoepeau
4	Norm Maxwell	4	'Isileli Fatani
5	Robin Brooke	5	Benhur Kivalu
6	Reuben Thorne	6	Vaohingano Fakatou
7	Josh Kronfeld	7	Sonatane Koloi
8	Taine Randell (c)	8	Va'a Toloke
16	Daryl Gibson *	16	Sione Mone Tu'ipulotu *
17	Carlos Spencer	17	'Isi Tapueluelu *
18	Byron Kelleher *	18	Falamani Mafi *
19	Andrew Blowers	19	David Edwards *
20	Royce Willis	20	Mat Te Pou *
21	Craig Dowd *	21	Ngalu Taufo'ou *
22	Mark Hammett	22	Taunaholo Taufahema *

Referee: Derek Bevan

Huddersfield 14.10.99

New Zealand 101	Italy 3
Tries: Wilson (3), Brown, Mika, Lomu (2), Osborne (2), Randell, Gibson, Robinson, Cullen, Hammett	Pens: Dominguez
Cons: Brown (11)	
Pens: Brown (3)	

	New Zealand		Italy
15	Jeff Wilson	15	Matt Pini
14	Glen Osborne	14	Paolo Vaccari
13	Pita Alatini	13	Christian Stoica
12	Daryl Gibson	12	Alessandro Ceppolino
11	Jonah Lomu	11	Nicolas Zisti
10	Tony Brown	10	Diego Dominguez
9	Byron Kelleher	9	Alessandro Troncon
1	Greg Feek	1	Alessandro Moreno
2	Mark Hammett	2	Andrea Moretti
3	Craig Dowd	3	Andrea Castellani
4	Ian Jones	4	Carlo Checchinato
5	Royce Willis	5	Mark Giacheri
6	Dylan Mika	6	Massimo Giovanelli (c)
7	Andrew Blowers	7	Stefano Saviozzi
8	Taine Randell (c)	8	Carlo Caione
16	Christian Cullen *	16	Nicola Mazzucato *
17	Andrew Mehrtens	17	Francesco Mazzariol *
18	Rhys Duggan *	18	Giampiero Mazzi
19	Scott Robertson *	19	Orazio Arancio *
20	Robin Brooke *	20	Valter Cristofoletto *
21	Kees Meeuws *	21	Franco Properzi-Curti *
22	Anton Oliver *	22	Alessandro Moscardi *

Referee: Jim Fleming

Murrayfield 8.10.99

Scotland 43	Uruguay 12
Tries: Armstrong, M Leslie, Metcalfe, Russell, Simpson, Townsend	Pens: D Aguirre (3), Sciarra
Cons: Logan (5)	
Pens: Logan	

	Scotland		Uruguay
15	Glenn Metcalfe	15	Alfonso Cardoso
14	Cameron Murray	14	Juan Menchaca
13	Alan Tait	13	Pedro Vecino
12	Jamie Mayer	12	Martin Mendaro
11	Kenny Logan	11	Pablo Costabile
10	Gregor Townsend	10	Diego Aguirre
9	Gary Armstrong (c)	9	Federico Sciarra
1	Tom Smith	1	Rodrigo Sanchez
2	Gordon Bulloch	2	Diego Lamelas
3	George Graham	3	Pablo Lemoine
4	Scott Murray	4	Juan Carlos Bado
5	Stuart Grimes	5	Mario Lame
6	Martin Leslie	6	Nicolas Brignoni
7	Budge Pountney	7	Martin Panizza
8	Gordon Simpson	8	Diego Ormaechea (c)
16	Shaun Longstaff *	16	Jose Viana *
17	Duncan Hodge	17	Fernando Sosa Diaz *
18	Bryan Redpath *	18	Nicolas Grille *
19	Peter Walton *	19	Eduardo Berruti *
20	Doddie Weir	20	Agustin Ponce de Leon *
21	David Hilton *	21	Guillermo Storace *
22	Robert Russell *	22	Francisco de los Santos *

Referee: Stuart Dickinson

Murrayfield 16.10.99

Scotland 48	Spain 0
Tries: Pen try, Mather (2), Longstaff, McLaren, C Murray, Hodge	
Cons: Hodge (5)	
Pens: Hodge	

	Scotland		Spain
15	Chris Paterson	15	Francisco Puertas
14	Cameron Murray	14	Jose Ignacio Inchausti
13	Jamie Mayer	13	Alvar Enciso (c)
12	James McLaren	12	Sebastian Loubsens
11	Shaun Longstaff	11	Miguel Angel Frechilla
10	Duncan Hodge	10	Andrei Kovalenco
9	Bryan Redpath	9	Aratz Gallastegui
1	David Hilton	1	Victor Torres
2	Robert Russell	2	Diego Zarzosa
3	Paul Burnell	3	Jose Ignacio Zapatero
4	Doddie Weir	4	Jose Miguel Villau
5	Andy Reed	5	Oskar Astarloa
6	Peter Walton	6	Jose Diaz
7	Cameron Mather	7	Carlos Souto
8	Stuart Reid	8	Alfonso Mata
16	Glenn Metcalfe	16	Ferran Velasco *
17	Gregor Townsend *	17	Alberto Socias *
18	Iain Fairley *	18	Jaime Alonso
19	Martin Leslie	19	Agustin Malet *
20	Stuart Grimes	20	Steve Tuineau *
21	George Graham	21	Luis Javier Martinez *
22	Gordon Bulloch	22	Fernando de la Calle *

Referee: Clayton Thomas

Twickenham 9.10.99

England 16	New Zealand 30
Tries: De Glanville	Tries: Wilson, Lomu, Kelleher
Cons: Wilkinson	Cons: Mehrtens (3)
Pens: Wilkinson (3)	Pens: Mehrtens (3)

	England		New Zealand
15	Matt Perry	15	Jeff Wilson
14	Austin Healey	14	Tana Umaga
13	Phil de Glanville	13	Christian Cullen
12	Jeremy Guscott	12	Alama Ieremia
11	Dan Luger	11	Jonah Lomu
10	Jonny Wilkinson	10	Andrew Mehrtens
9	Matt Dawson	9	Justin Marshall
1	Jason Leonard	1	Carl Hoeft
2	Richard Cockerill	2	Anton Oliver
3	Phil Vickery	3	Craig Dowd
4	Martin Johnson (c)	4	Norm Maxwell
5	Danny Grewcock	5	Robin Brooke
6	Richard Hill	6	Reuben Thorne
7	Neil Back	7	Josh Kronfeld
8	Lawrence Dallaglio	8	Taine Randell (c)
16	Nick Beal *	16	Daryl Gibson *
17	Will Greenwood	17	Tony Brown *
18	Paul Grayson *	18	Byron Kelleher *
19	Martin Corry *	19	Andrew Blowers
20	Tim Rodber *	20	Royce Willis *
21	Darren Garforth *	21	Greg Feek *
22	Phil Greening *	22	Mark Hammett

Referee: Peter Marshall

Twickenham 15.10.99

England 101	Tonga 10
Tries: Dawson, Greening (2), Luger (2), Perry, Greenwood (2), Healey (2), Hill, Guscott (2)	Tries: Tiueti
Cons: Grayson (12)	Cons: S Tu'ipulotu
Pens: Grayson (4)	Pens: S Tu'ipulotu

	England		Tonga
15	Matt Perry	15	Sateki Tu'ipulotu
14	Austin Healey	14	Tevita Tiueti
13	Will Greenwood	13	Fepi'kou Tatafu
12	Jeremy Guscott	12	Salesi Finau
11	Dan Luger	11	Semi Taupeaafe
10	Paul Grayson	10	'Elisi Vunipola (c)
9	Matt Dawson	9	Sililo Martens
1	Graham Rowntree	1	Ngalu Taufo'ou
2	Phil Greening	2	Fe'ao Vunipola
3	Phil Vickery	3	Tevita Taumoepeau
4	Martin Johnson (c)	4	'Isileli Fatani
5	Garath Archer	5	Benhur Kivalu
6	Joe Worsley	6	David Edwards
7	Richard Hill	7	Sonatane Koloi
8	Lawrence Dallaglio	8	Katilimoni Tu'ipulotu
16	Nick Beal *	16	Falamani Mafi *
17	Mike Catt *	17	'Isi Tapueluelu *
18	Jonny Wilkinson *	18	'Epeli Taione *
19	Neil Back *	19	Sione Mone Tu'ipulotu *
20	Danny Grewcock *	20	Va'a Toloke *
21	Jason Leonard *	21	Ta'u Fa'inga'anuku *
22	Richard Cockerill *	22	Latiume Maka *

Referee: Wayne Erickson

Pool C

Béziers 1.10.99

Fiji 67	Namibia 18
Tries: Lasagavibau (2), Tiko, Katalau, Tawake, Satala, Mocelutu, Smith, Rauluni	Tries: Senekal, Jacobs
Cons: Serevi (8)	Cons: Van Dyk
Pens: Serevi (2)	Pens: Van Dyk (2)
15 Alfred Uluinayau	15 Leandre van Dyk
14 Fero Lasagavibau	14 Dirk Farmer
13 Viliame Satala	13 Arthur Samuelson
12 Waisake Sotutu	12 Schalk van der Merwe
11 Imanueli Tikomaimakogai	11 Deon Mouton
10 Waisale Serevi	10 Johan Zaayman
9 Jacob Rauluni	9 Riaan Jantjies
1 Dan Rouse	1 Mario Jacobs
2 Greg Smith (c)	2 Hugo Horn
3 Joeli Veitayaki	3 Gerhard Opperman
4 Simon Raiwalui	4 Heino Senekal
5 Emori Katalau	5 Pieter Steyn
6 Apenisa Naevo	6 Quinn Hough (c)
7 Setareki Tawake	7 Jaco Olivier
8 Alivereti Mocelutu	8 Sean Furter
16 Mosese Rauluni	16 Glovin van Wyk *
17 Nicky Little *	17 F. Janse van Rensburg *
18 Meli Nakauta *	18 S. Janse van Rensburg *
19 Kolinio Sewabu *	19 Herman Lintvelt *
20 Ifereimi Tawake	20 Johannes Theron *
21 Epeli Naituivau *	21 Andries Blaauw *
22 Isaia Rasila	22 Eben Smith *

Referee: David McHugh

Béziers 2.10.99

France 33	Canada 20
Tries: Glas, Magne, T Castaignede, Ntamack	Tries: Williams (2)
Cons: Dourthe (2)	Cons: Rees, Ross
Pens: Dourthe (3)	Pens: Rees, Ross
15 Ugo Mola	15 Scott Stewart
14 Xavier Garbajosa	14 Winston Stanley
13 Richard Dourthe	13 David Lougheed
12 Stephane Glas	12 Scott Bryan
11 Christophe Dominici	11 Courtney Smith
10 Thomas Castaignede	10 Gareth Rees (c)
9 Pierre Mignoni	9 Morgan Williams
1 Christian Califano	1 Rod Snow
2 Raphael Ibanez (c)	2 Pat Dunkley
3 Franck Tournaire	3 Jon Thiel
4 Abdelatif Benazzi	4 John Tait
5 Fabien Pelous	5 Mike James
6 Marc Lievremont	6 John Hutchinson
7 Olivier Magne	7 Danny Baugh
8 Christophe Juillet	8 Al Charron
16 Emile Ntamack *	16 Kyle Nichols
17 Christophe Lamaison *	17 Bobby Ross *
18 Stephane Castaignede *	18 John Graf *
19 Lionel Mallier *	19 Mike Schmid *
20 Olivier Brouzet *	20 Ryan Banks *
21 Cedric Soulette *	21 Richard Bice *
22 Marc Dal Maso	22 Mark Cardinal

Referee: Brian Campsall

Bordeaux 8.10.99

France 47	Namibia 13
Tries: Mola (3), Mignoni, Bernat-Salles, Ntamack	Tries: Samuelson
Cons: Dourthe (4)	Cons: Van Dyk
Pens: Dourthe (3)	Pens: Van Dyyk (2)
15 Ugo Mola	15 Glovin van Wyk
14 Philippe Bernat-Salles	14 Leandre van Dyk
13 Richard Dourthe	13 F. Janse van Rensburg
12 Stephane Glas	12 Schalk van Der Merwe
11 Emile Ntamack	11 Arthur Samuelson
10 Christophe Lamaison	10 Johan Zaayman
9 Pierre Mignoni	9 Riaan Jantjies
1 Christian Califano	1 Mario Jacobs
2 Raphael Ibanez (c)	2 Hugo Horn
3 Franck Tournaire	3 Gerhard Opperman
4 Olivier Brouzet	4 Heino Senekal
5 Fabien Pelous	5 Pieter Steyn
6 Marc Lievremont	6 Quinn Hough (c)
7 Olivier Magne	7 Mathys van Rooyen
8 Thomas Lievremont	8 Sean Furter
16 Cedric Desbrosse *	16 Rock Loubser *
17 Xavier Garbajosa *	17 Lukas Holtzhausen
18 Stephane Castaignede *	18 S. Janse van Rensburg *
19 Arnaud Costes *	19 Johannes Theron *
20 Abdelatif Benazzi *	20 Herman Lintvelt *
21 Cedric Soulette *	21 Andries Blaauw *
22 Marc Dal Maso *	22 Eben Smith *

Referee: Chris White

Bordeaux 9.10.99

Fiji 38	Canada 22
Tries: Satala (2), Vunibaka, pen try	Tries: James
Cons: Little (3)	Cons: Rees
Pens: Little (3)	Pens: Rees (4)
DG: Little	DG: Rees
15 Alfred Uluinayau	15 Scott Stewart
14 Fero Lasagavibau	14 Winston Stanley
13 Viliame Satala	13 Kyle Nichols
12 Waisake Sotutu	12 Scott Bryan
11 Marika Vunibaka	11 David Lougheed
10 Nicky Little	10 Gareth Rees (c)
9 Jacob Rauluni	9 Morgan Williams
1 Dan Rouse	1 Rod Snow
2 Greg Smith (c)	2 Pat Dunkley
3 Joeli Veitayaki	3 Jon Thiel
4 Simon Raiwalui	4 John Tait
5 Emori Katalau	5 Mike James
6 Ilie Tabua	6 Al Charron
7 Setareki Tawake	7 Danny Baugh
8 Alivereti Mocelutu	8 Mike Schmid
16 Mosese Rauluni *	16 Joe Pagano
17 Waisale Serevi *	17 Bobby Ross
18 Meli Nakauta	18 John Graf
19 Kolinio Sewabu *	19 Ryan Banks
20 Apenisa Naevo *	20 John Hutchinson *
21 Niko Qoro	21 Duane Major *
22 Isaia Rasila	22 Mark Cardinal *

Referee: Ed Morrison

Toulouse 14.10.99

Canada 72	Namibia 11
Tries: Nichols (2), Snow (2), Stanley (2), Charron, Ross, Williams	Tries: Hough
Cons: Rees (9)	Pens: Van Dyk (2)
Pens: Rees (3)	
15 Scott Stewart	15 Glovin van Wyk
14 Winston Stanley	14 Leandre van Dyk
13 David Lougheed	13 F. Janse van Rensburg
12 Kyle Nichols	12 Schalk van Der Merwe
11 Joe Pagano	11 Arthur Samuelson
10 Gareth Rees	10 Johan Zaayman
9 Morgan Williams	9 Riaan Jantjies
1 Rod Snow	1 Eben Smith
2 Mark Cardinal	2 Hugo Horn
3 Jon Thiel	3 Gerhard Opperman
4 John Tait	4 Heino Senekal
5 Mike James	5 Pieter Steyn
6 John Hutchinson	6 Quinn Hough
7 Danny Baugh	7 Mathys van Rooyen
8 Al Charron	8 Sean Furter
16 Scott Bryan *	16 Dirk Farmer
17 Bobby Ross *	17 Lukas Holtzhausen
18 John Graf *	18 Ronaldo Pedro
19 Mike Schmid *	19 Herman Lintvelt *
20 Ryan Banks *	20 Johannes Theron *
21 Duane Major *	21 Frans Fisch
22 Pat Dunkley *	22 Andries Blaauw *

Referee: Andrew Cole

Toulouse 16.10.99

France 28	Fiji 19
Tries: Juillet, pen try, Dominici	Tries: Uluinayau
Cons: Dourthe (2)	Cons: Little
Pens: Dourthe (2) Lamaison	Pens: Little (4)
15 Ugo Mola	15 Alfred Uluinayau
14 Philippe Bernat-Salles	14 Fero Lasagavibau
13 Richard Dourthe	13 Viliame Satala
12 Emile Ntamack	12 Meli Nakauta
11 Christophe Dominici	11 Manasa Bari
10 Christophe Lamaison	10 Waisale Serevi
9 Stephane Castaignede	9 Jacob Rauluni
1 Cedric Soulette	1 Dan Rouse
2 Raphael Ibanez (c)	2 Greg Smith (c)
3 Franck Tournaire	3 Joeli Veitayaki
4 Abdelatif Benazzi	4 Simon Raiwalui
5 Fabien Pelous	5 Emori Katalau
6 Marc Lievremont	6 Ilie Tabua
7 Olivier Magne	7 Setareki Tawake
8 Christophe Juillet	8 Alivereti Mocelutu
16 Xavier Garbajosa *	16 Mosese Rauluni
17 Cedric Desbrosse	17 Nicky Little
18 Fabien Galthie *	18 Waisake Sotutu *
19 Arnaud Costes *	19 Kolinio Sewabu *
20 Olivier Brouzet *	20 Ifereimi Tawake
21 Pieter de Villiers	21 Epeli Naituivau
22 Marc Dal Maso *	22 Isaia Rasila

Referee: Paddy O'Brien

Pool D

Cardiff 1.10.99

Wales 23	Argentina 18
Tries: Charvis, Taylor	Pens: Quesada (6)
Cons: N Jenkins (2)	
Pens: N Jenkins (3)	
15 Shane Howarth	15 Manuel Contepomi
14 Gareth Thomas	14 Octavio Bartolucci
13 Mark Taylor	13 Eduardo Simone
12 Scott Gibbs	12 Lisandro Arbizu (c)
11 Dafydd James	11 Diego Albanese
10 Neil Jenkins	10 Gonzalo Quesada
9 Rob Howley (c)	9 Agustin Pichot
1 Peter Rogers	1 Roberto Grau
2 Garin Jenkins	2 Mario Ledesma
3 David Young	3 Mauricio Reggiardo
4 Craig Quinnell	4 Ignacio Fernandez Lobbe
5 Chris Wyatt	5 Alejandro Allub
6 Colin Charvis	6 Santiago Phelan
7 Brett Sinkinson	7 Lucas Ostiglia
8 Scott Quinnell	8 Gonzalo Longo
16 Jason Jones-Hughes *	16 Gonzalo Camardon *
17 Stephen Jones	17 Felipe Contepomi
18 David Llewellyn	18 N. Fernandez Miranda
19 Mike Voyle	19 Raul Perez
20 Ben Evans	20 Rolando Martin *
21 Andrew Lewis	21 Omar Hasan *
22 Jonathan Humphreys	22 Agustin Canalda

Referee: Paddy O'Brien

Wrexham 3.10.99

Samoa 43	Japan 9
Tries: Lima (2), So'oalo (2), Leaega	Pens: Hirose (3)
Cons: Leaega (3)	
Pens: Leaega (4)	
15 Silao Leaega	15 Tsutomu Matsuda
14 Afato So'oalo	14 Daisuke Ohata
13 To'o Vaega	13 Andrew McCormick (c)
12 Va'aiga Tuigamala	12 Yukio Motoki
11 Brian Lima	11 Terunori Masuho
10 Stephen Bachop	10 Keiji Hirose
9 Steven So'oialo	9 Graeme Bachop
1 Brendan Reidy	1 Shin Hasegawa
2 Trevor Leota	2 Masahiro Kunda
3 Robbie Ale	3 Kohei Oguchi
4 Sene Ta'ala	4 Rob Gordon
5 Lama Tone	5 Naoya Okubo
6 Junior Paramore	6 Yasunori Watanabe
7 Craig Glendinning	7 Greg Smith
8 Pat Lam (c)	8 Jamie Joseph
16 George Leaupepe *	16 Pat Tuidrake *
17 Earl Va'a *	17 Akira Yoshida *
18 Jon Clarke *	18 Wataru Murata
19 Semo Sititi *	19 Takeomi Ito *
20 Opeta Palepoi *	20 Hiroyuki Tanuma *
21 Mike Mika *	21 Toshikazu Nakamichi
22 Onehunga Matauiau	22 Masaaki Sakata *

Referee: Andrew Cole

Cardiff 9.10.99

Wales 64	Japan 15
Tries: Taylor (2), Bateman, Howley, Gibbs, Howarth, D Llewellyn, Thomas, pen try	Tries: Ohata, Tuidraki
Cons: N Jenkins (8)	Cons: Hirose
Pens: N Jenkins	Pens: Hirose
15 Shane Howarth	15 Tsuyoshi Hirao
14 Jason Jones-Hughes	14 Daisuke Ohata
13 Mark Taylor	13 Andrew McCormick (c)
12 Scott Gibbs	12 Yukio Motoki
11 Allan Bateman	11 Pat Tuidrake
10 Neil Jenkins	10 Keiji Hirose
9 Rob Howley (c)	9 Graeme Bachop
1 Peter Rogers	1 Shin Hasegawa
2 Garin Jenkins	2 Masahiro Kunda
3 David Young	3 Naoto Nakamura
4 Craig Quinnell	4 Rob Gordon
5 Mike Voyle	5 Hiroyuki Tanuma
6 Martyn Williams	6 Naoya Okubo
7 Brett Sinkinson	7 Greg Smith
8 Geraint Lewis	8 Jamie Joseph
16 Stephen Jones *	16 Terunori Masuho
17 Gareth Thomas *	17 Akira Yoshida
18 David Llewellyn *	18 Wataru Murata *
19 Chris Wyatt *	19 Takeomi Ito *
20 Ben Evans *	20 Yoshihiko Sakuraba *
21 Andrew Lewis *	21 Toshikazu Nakamichi *
22 Jonathan Humphreys *	22 Masaaki Sakata *

Referee: Joel Dume

Llanelli 10.10.99

Argentina 32	Samoa 16
Tries: Allub	Tries: Paramore
Pens: Quesada (8)	Cons: Leaega
DG: Quesada	Pens: Leaega (3)
15 Manuel Contepomi	15 Silao Leaega
14 Octavio Bartolucci	14 Afato So'oalo
13 Eduardo Simone	13 George Leaupepe
12 Lisandro Arbizu	12 Va'aiga Tuigamala
11 Diego Albanese	11 Brian Lima
10 Gonzalo Quesada	10 Stephen Bachop
9 Agustin Pichot	9 Steven So'oialo
1 Mauricio Reggiardo	1 Brendan Reidy
2 Mario Ledesma	2 Trevor Leota
3 Omar Hasan	3 Robbie Ale
4 Ignacio Fernandez Lobbe	4 Opeta Palepoi
5 Alejandro Allub	5 Lama Tone
6 Santiago Phelan	6 Sene Ta'ala
7 Rolando Martin	7 Junior Paramore
8 Gonzalo Longo	8 Pat Lam
16 Gonzalo Camardon *	16 To'o Vaega *
17 Felipe Contepomi	17 Tanner Vili *
18 N. Fernandez Miranda	18 Jon Clarke
19 Miguel Ruiz *	19 Kalolo Toleafoa *
20 Lucas Ostiglia	20 Isaac Feaunati *
21 Martin Scelzo *	21 Mike Mika *
22 Agustin Canalda	22 Onehunga Matauiau *

Referee: Wayne Erickson

Cardiff 14.10.99

Wales 31	Samoa 38
Tries: Pen try (2), Thomas	Tries: Bachop (2), Falaniko, Lam, Leaega
Cons: N Jenkins (2)	Cons: Leaega (5)
Pens: N Jenkins (4)	Pens: Leaega
15 Shane Howarth	15 Silao Leaega
14 Gareth Thomas	14 Brian Lima
13 Mark Taylor	13 To'o Vaega
12 Scott Gibbs	12 George Leaupepe
11 Dafydd James	11 Va'aiga Tuigamala
10 Neil Jenkins	10 Stephen Bachop
9 Rob Howley (c)	9 Steven So'oialo
1 Peter Rogers	1 Brendan Reidy
2 Garin Jenkins	2 Trevor Leota
3 David Young	3 Robbie Ale
4 Gareth Llewellyn	4 Lio Falaniko
5 Chris Wyatt	5 Lama Tone
6 Martyn Williams	6 Junior Paramore
7 Brett Sinkinson	7 Craig Glendinning
8 Scott Quinnell	8 Pat Lam (c)
16 Stephen Jones	16 Terry Fanolua *
17 Jason Jones-Hughes	17 Earl Va'a *
18 David Llewellyn	18 Jon Clarke
19 Geraint Lewis	19 Semo Sititi *
20 Mike Voyle	20 Sene Ta'ala *
21 Ben Evans *	21 Mike Mika *
22 Andrew Lewis *	22 Onehunga Matauiau *

Referee: Ed Morrison

Cardiff 16.10.99

Argentina 33	Japan 12
Tries: Pichot, Albanese	Penss: Hirose (4)
Cons: Contepomi	
Pens: Quesada (7)	
15 Ignacio Corletto	15 Tsutomu Matsuda
14 Gonzalo Camardon	14 Daisuke Ohata
13 Eduardo Simone	13 Andrew McCormick
12 Lisandro Arbizu	12 Yukio Motoki
11 Diego Albanese	11 Pat Tuidrake
10 Gonzalo Quesada	10 Keiji Hirose
9 Agustin Pichot	9 Graeme Bachop
1 Mauricio Reggiardo	1 Toshikazu Nakamichi
2 Mario Ledesma	2 Masahiro Kunda
3 Omar Hasan	3 Kohei Oguchi
4 Pedro Sporleder	4 Rob Gordon
5 Alejandro Allub	5 Hiroyuki Tanuma
6 Santiago Phelan	6 Naoya Okubo
7 Rolando Martin	7 Greg Smith
8 Ignacio Fernandez Lobbe	8 Jamie Joseph
16 Jose Orengo	16 Terunori Masuho
17 Felipe Contepomi *	17 Takeomi Ito *
18 N. Fernandez Miranda	18 Wataru Murata
19 Miguel Ruiz *	19 Yoshihiko Sakuraba *
20 Lucas Ostiglia *	20 Naoto Nakamura *
21 Agustin Canalda	21 Shin Hasegawa *
22 Martin Scelzo	22 Masaaki Sakata *

Referee: Stuart Dickinson

Pool E

Dublin 2.10.99

Ireland 53	United States 8
Tries: Wood (4), Bishop, O'Driscoll, pen try	Tries: Dalzell
Cons: Humphreys (4), Elwood (2)	Pens: Dalzell
Pens: Humphreys (2)	

15 Conor O'Shea	15 Kurt Shuman
14 Justin Bishop	14 Vaea Anitoni
13 Brian O'Driscoll	13 Juan Grobler
12 Kevin Maggs	12 Tomasi Takau
11 Matthew Mostyn	11 Brian Hightower
10 David Humphreys	10 Mark Williams
9 Thomas Tierney	9 Kevin Dalzell
1 Peter Clohessy	1 George Sucher
2 Keith Wood	2 Tom Billups
3 Paul Wallace	3 Ray Lehner
4 Paddy Johns	4 Luke Gross
5 Jeremy Davidson	5 Alec Parker
6 Trevor Brennan	6 Dave Hodges
7 Andy Ward	7 Richard Tardits
8 Dion O'Cuinneagain (c)	8 Dan Lyle (c)
16 Jonathan Bell *	16 Mark Scharrenberg *
17 Eric Elwood *	17 David Niu *
18 Brian O'Meara *	18 Jesse Coulson
19 Eric Miller *	19 Tasi Mo'unga *
20 Malcolm O'Kelly *	20 Shaun Paga *
21 Justin Fitzpatrick *	21 Joe Clayton
22 Ross Nesdale *	22 Kirk Khasigian *

Referee: Joel Dume

Belfast 3.10.99

Australia 57	Romania 9
Tries: Kefu (3), Roff (2), Burke, Horan, Little, Paul	Pens: Mitu (3)
Cons: Burke (5), Eales	

15 Matthew Burke	15 Mihai Vioreanu
14 Ben Tune	14 Cristian Sauan
13 Daniel Herbert	13 Gabriel Brezoianu
12 Tim Horan	12 Romeo Gontineac
11 Jason Little	11 Gheorghe Solomie
10 Rod Kafer	10 Lucien Roland Vusec
9 George Gregan	9 Petre Mitu
1 Richard Harry	1 Stan Constantin
2 Phil Kearns	2 Petru Balan
3 Andrew Blades	3 Laurentiu Rotaru
4 David Giffin	4 Tiberiu Brinza
5 John Eales	5 Ovidiu Slusariuc
6 Owen Finegan	6 Adrian Alin Petrache
7 David Wilson	7 Erdinci Septar
8 Toutai Kefu	8 Catalin Draguceanu
16 Joe Roff *	16 Marius Iacob
17 Nathan Grey *	17 Ionut Tofan
18 Chris Whitaker *	18 Radu Fugigi
19 Tiaan Strauss *	19 Florin Corodeanu *
20 Mark Connors	20 Daniel Chiriac *
21 Dan Crowley *	21 Nicole Dragos Dima *
22 Jeremy Paul *	22 Razvan Mavrodin *

Referee: Paul Honiss

Dublin 9.10.99

United States 25	Romania 27
Tries: Lyle, Hightower, Shuman	Tries: Solomie (2), Constantin, Petrache
Cons: Dalzell (2)	Cons: Mitu (2)
Pens: Dalzell (2)	Pens: Mitu

15 Kurt Shuman	15 Mihai Vioreanu
14 Vaea Anitoni	14 Cristian Sauan
13 Juan Grobler	13 Gabriel Brezoianu
12 Mark Scharrenberg	12 Romeo Gontineac
11 Brian Hightower	11 Gheorghe Solomie
10 David Niu	10 Lucien Roland Vusec
9 Kevin Dalzell	9 Petre Mitu
1 George Sucher	1 Razvan Mavrodin
2 Tom Billups	2 Petru Balan
3 Ray Lehner	3 Constantin Stan
4 Luke Gross	4 Tiberiu Brinza (c)
5 Alec Parker	5 Tudor Constantin
6 Dan Lyle (c)	6 Adrian Alin Petrache
7 Tasi Mo'unga	7 Erdinci Septar
8 Rob Lumkong	8 Catalin Draguceanu
16 Joe Clayton *	16 Marius Iacob
17 Tomasi Takau *	17 Ionut Tofan
18 David Stroble	18 Radu Fugigi
19 Shaun Paga *	19 Florin Corodeanu *
20 Dave Hodges *	20 Daniel Chiriac *
21 Richard Tardits *	21 Nicole Dragos Dima *
22 Kirk Khasigian *	22 Stefan Demci

Referee: Jim Fleming

Dublin 10.10.99

Ireland 3	Australia 23
Pens: Humphreys	Tries: Horan, Tune
	Cons: Burke (2)
	Pens: Burke (2), Eales

15 Conor O'Shea	15 Matthew Burke
14 Justin Bishop	14 Ben Tune
13 Brian O'Driscoll	13 Daniel Herbert
12 Kevin Maggs	12 Tim Horan
11 Matthew Mostyn	11 Joe Roff
10 David Humphreys	10 Stephen Larkham
9 Thomas Tierney	9 George Gregan
1 Justin Fitzpatrick	1 Richard Harry
2 Keith Wood	2 Phil Kearns
3 Paul Wallace	3 Andrew Blades
4 Paddy Johns	4 David Giffin
5 Malcolm O'Kelly	5 John Eales (c)
6 Trevor Brennan	6 Mark Connors
7 Andy Ward	7 David Wilson
8 Dion O'Cuinneagain (c)	8 Toutai Kefu
16 Jonathan Bell *	16 Jason Little *
17 Eric Elwood *	17 Nathan Grey *
18 Brian O'Meara	18 Chris Whitaker
19 Eric Miller *	19 Tiaan Strauss *
20 Robert Casey *	20 Owen Finegan *
21 Peter Clohessy *	21 Dan Crowley *
22 Ross Nesdale *	22 Jeremy Paul *

Referee: Clayton Thomas

Limerick 14.10.99

Australia 55	United States 19
Tries: Staniforth (2), Burke, Foley, Larkham, Latham, Strauss, Whitaker	Tries: Grobler
Cons: Burke (5), Roff	Cons: Dalzell
Pens: Burke	Pens: Dalzell (3)
	DG: Niu

15 Chris Latham	15 Kurt Shuman
14 Scott Staniforth	14 Vaea Anitoni
13 Jason Little	13 Juan Grobler
12 Nathan Grey	12 Mark Scharrenberg
11 Matthew Burke	11 Brian Hightower
10 Stephen Larkham	10 David Niu
9 Chris Whitaker	9 Kevin Dalzell
1 Dan Crowley	1 Joe Clayton
2 Michael Foley	2 Tom Billups
3 Rod Moore	3 George Sucher
4 Mark Connors	4 Luke Gross
5 Tom Bowman	5 Alec Parker
6 Owen Finegan	6 Dave Hodges
7 Tiaan Strauss	7 Tasi Mo'unga
8 Jim Williams	8 Rob Lumkong
16 Joe Roff *	16 Tomasi Takau *
17 Rod Kafer *	17 Alatini Saulala *
18 George Gregan	18 Jesse Coulson *
19 Matt Cockbain *	19 Shaun Paga *
20 David Giffin *	20 Eric Reed *
21 Richard Harry	21 Marc L'Huillier *
22 Jeremy Paul	22 Kirk Khasigian *

Referee: Andre Watson

Dublin 15.10.99

Ireland 44	Romania 14
Tries: O'Shea (2), O'Cuinneagain, Tierney, Ward	Tries: Sauan
Cons: Elwood (5)	Pens: Mitu (3)
Pens: Elwood (2)	
DG: O'Driscoll	

15 Conor O'Shea	15 Mihai Vioreanu
14 James Topping	14 Cristian Sauan
13 Jonathan Bell	13 Gabriel Brezoianu
12 Michael Mullins	12 Romeo Gontineac
11 Matthew Mostyn	11 Gheorghe Solomie
10 Eric Elwood	10 Lucien Roland Vusec
9 Thomas Tierney	9 Petre Mitu
1 Justin Fitzpatrick	1 Razvan Mavrodin
2 Ross Nesdale	2 Petru Balan
3 Paul Wallace	3 Constantin Stan
4 Paddy Johns	4 Tudor Constantin (c)
5 Malcolm O'Kelly	5 Tiberiu Brinza
6 Andy Ward	6 Adrian Alin Petrache
7 Kieron Dawson	7 Erdinci Septar
8 Dion O'Cuinneagain (c)	8 Catalin Draguceanu
16 Gordon D'Arcy *	16 Marius Iacob *
17 Brian O'Driscoll *	17 Ionut Tofan *
18 Brian O'Meara *	18 Radu Fugigi *
19 Alan Quinlan *	19 Florin Corodeanu *
20 Jeremy Davidson *	20 Daniel Chiriac *
21 Angus McKeen *	21 Nicole Dragos Dima *
22 Keith Wood *	22 Laurentiu Rotaru *

Referee: Brian Campsall

Final Pool Tables

POOL A

	W	D	L	F	A	Pts
South Africa	3	0	0	132	35	9
Scotland	2	0	1	120	58	7
Uruguay	1	0	2	42	97	5
Spain	0	0	3	18	122	3

POOL B

	W	D	L	F	A	Pts
New Zealand	3	0	0	176	28	9
England	2	0	1	184	47	7
Tonga	1	0	2	47	171	5
Italy	0	0	3	35	196	3

POOL C

	W	D	L	F	A	Pts
France	3	0	0	108	52	9
Fiji	2	0	1	124	68	7
Canada	1	0	2	114	82	5
Namibia	0	0	3	42	186	3

POOL D

	W	D	L	F	A	Pts
Wales	2	0	1	118	71	7
Samoa	2	0	1	97	72	7
Argentina	2	0	1	83	51	7
Japan	0	0	3	36	140	3

POOL E

	W	D	L	F	A	Pts
Australia	3	0	0	135	31	9
Ireland	2	0	1	100	45	7
Romania	1	0	2	50	126	5
United States	0	0	3	52	135	3

Third Best Overall

	W	D	L	F	A	Pts
Argentina	2	0	1	83	51	7
Canada	1	0	2	114	82	5
Romania	1	0	2	50	126	5
Tonga	1	0	2	47	171	5
Uruguay	1	0	2	42	97	5

Quarter-Final Play-Offs

Twickenham 20.10.99

England 45	Fiji 24
Tries: Luger, Back, Beal, Greening	Tries: Satala, Tikomaimakogai, Nakauta
Cons: Wilkinson, Dawson	Cons: Little (3)
Pens: Wilkinson (7)	Pens: Serevi

15 Matt Perry	15 Alfred Uluinayau
14 Nick Beal	14 Marika Vunibaka
13 Will Greenwood	13 Viliame Satala
12 Mike Catt	12 Meli Nakauta
11 Dan Luger	11 Imanueli Tikomaimakogai
10 Jonny Wilkinson	10 Waisale Serevi
9 Austin Healey	9 Mosese Rauluni
1 Jason Leonard	1 Dan Rouse
2 Phil Greening	2 Greg Smith (c)
3 Darren Garforth	3 Joeli Veitayaki
4 Martin Johnson (c)	4 Simon Raiwalui
5 Garath Archer	5 Emori Katalau
6 Joe Worsley	6 Kolinio Sewabu
7 Neil Back	7 Setareki Tawake
8 Lawrence Dallaglio	8 Ifereimi Tawake
16 Phil de Glanville *	16 Jacob Rauluni *
17 Paul Grayson *	17 Nicky Little *
18 Matt Dawson *	18 Waisake Sototu *
19 Richard Hill *	19 Inoke Male *
20 Tim Rodber *	20 Ratu Alifereti Doviverata
21 Graham Rowntree *	21 Epeli Naituivau *
22 Richard Cockerill *	22 Isaia Rasila *

Referee: Clayton Thomas

Murrayfield 20.10.99

Scotland 35	Samoa 20
Tries: Pen try, M Leslie, C Murray	Tries: Sititi, Lima
Cons: Logan	Cons: Leaega (2)
Pens: Logan (5)	Pens: Leaega (2)
DG: Townsend	

15 Glenn Metcalfe	15 Silao Leaega
14 Cameron Murray	14 Brian Lima
13 Jamie Mayer	13 To'o Vaega
12 James McLaren	12 Terry Fanolua
11 Kenny Logan	11 Va'aiga Tuigamala
10 Gregor Townsend	10 Stephen Bachop
9 Gary Armstrong (c)	9 Steven So'oialo
1 Tom Smith	1 Brendan Reidy
2 Gordon Bulloch	2 Trevor Leota
3 George Graham	3 Samuela Asi
4 Scott Murray	4 Lio Falaniko
5 Doddie Weir	5 Lama Tone
6 Martin Leslie	6 Semo Sititi
7 Budge Pountney	7 Craig Glendinning
8 Gordon Simpson	8 Pat Lam (c)
16 Alan Tait	16 Filipo Toala *
17 Duncan Hodge *	17 Earl Va'a *
18 Bryan Redpath	18 Jon Clarke
19 Cameron Mather *	19 Isaac Feaunati
20 Stuart Grimes *	20 Sene Ta'ala *
21 Paul Burnell *	21 Robbie Ale *
22 Robert Russell *	22 Onehunga Matauiau *

Referee: David McHugh

Lens 20.10.99

Ireland 24	Argentina 28
Pens: Humphreys (7)	Tries: Albanese
DG: Humphreys	Cons: Quesada
	Pens: Quesada (7)

15 Conor O'Shea	15 Ignacio Corletto
14 Justin Bishop	14 Gonzalo Camardon
13 Brian O'Driscoll	13 Eduardo Simone
12 Kevin Maggs	12 Lisandro Arbizu (c)
11 Matthew Mostyn	11 Diego Albanese
10 David Humphreys	10 Gonzalo Quesada
9 Thomas Tierney	9 Agustin Pichot
1 Reggie Corrigan	1 Mauricio Reggiardo
2 Keith Wood	2 Mario Ledesma
3 Paul Wallace	3 Omar Hasan
4 Jeremy Davidson	4 Ignacio Fernandez Lobbe
5 Malcolm O'Kelly	5 Alejandro Allub
6 Andy Ward	6 Santiago Phelan
7 Kieron Dawson	7 Rolando Martin
8 Dion O'Cuinneagain (c)	8 Gonzalo Longo
16 Jonathan Bell	16 Manuel Contepomi
17 Eric Elwood	17 Felipe Contepomi *
18 Brian O'Meara	18 N. Fernandez Miranda
19 Eric Miller *	19 Lucas Ostiglia
20 Robert Casey *	20 Miguel Ruiz
21 Justin Fitzpatrick *	21 Agustin Canalda
22 Ross Nesdale	22 Martin Scelzo *

Referee: Stuart Dickinson

Cardiff 23.10.99

Wales 9
Pens: N Jenkins (3)

Australia 24
Tries: Gregan (2), Tune
Cons: Burke (3)
Pens: Burke

15	Shane Howarth	15	Matthew Burke
14	Gareth Thomas	14	Ben Tune
13	Mark Taylor	13	Daniel Herbert
12	Scott Gibbs	12	Tim Horan
11	Dafydd James	11	Joe Roff
10	Neil Jenkins	10	Stephen Larkham
9	Rob Howley (c)	9	George Gregan
1	Peter Rogers	1	Richard Harry
2	Garin Jenkins	2	Michael Foley
3	David Young	3	Andrew Blades
4	Craig Quinnell	4	David Giffin
5	Chris Wyatt	5	John Eales (c)
6	Colin Charvis	6	Matt Cockbain
7	Brett Sinkinson	7	David Wilson
8	Scott Quinnell	8	Tiaan Strauss
16	Stephen Jones	16	Jason Little *
17	Allan Bateman *	17	Nathan Grey
18	David Llewellyn	18	Chris Whitaker
19	Mike Voyle *	19	Mark Connors *
20	Ben Evans *	20	Owen Finegan *
21	Andrew Lewis *	21	Dan Crowley
22	Jonathan Humphreys	22	Jeremy Paul *

Referee: Colin Hawke

Dublin 24.10.99

France 47
Tries: Garbajosa (2),
Bernat-Salles (2), Ntamack
Cons: Lamaison (5)
Pens: Lamaison (4)

Argentina 26
Tries: Pichot, Arbizu
Cons: Quesada (2)
Pens: Quesada (3),
Contepomi

15	Xavier Garbajosa	15	Ignacio Corletto
14	Philippe Bernat-Salles	14	Gonzalo Camardon
13	Richard Dourthe	13	Eduardo Simone
12	Emile Ntamack	12	Lisandro Arbizu (c)
11	Christophe Dominici	11	Diego Albanese
10	Christophe Lamaison	10	Gonzalo Quesada
9	Fabien Galthie	9	Agustin Pichot
1	Cedric Soulette	1	Roberto Grau
2	Raphael Ibanez	2	Mario Ledesma
3	Franck Tournaire	3	Mauricio Reggiardo
4	Abdelatif Benazzi	4	Ignacio Fernandez Lobbe
5	Olivier Brouzet	5	Alejandro Allub
6	Marc Lievremont	6	Santiago Phelan
7	Olivier Magne	7	Rolando Martin
8	Christophe Juillet	8	Gonzalo Longo
16	Ugo Mola *	16	Manuel Contepomi *
17	Stephane Glas *	17	Felipe Contepomi *
18	Stephane Castaignede *	18	N. Fernandez Miranda *
19	Arnaud Costes *	19	Lucas Ostiglia *
20	David Auradou *	20	Miguel Ruiz *
21	Pieter de Villiers *	21	Agustin Canalda *
22	Marc Dal Maso *	22	Martin Scelzo *

Referee: Derek Bevan

Twickenham 30.10.99

South Africa 21
Pens: De Beer (6)
DG: De Beer

Australia 27 (aet)
Pens: Burke (8)
DG: Larkham

15	Percy Montgomery	15	Matthew Burke
14	Deon Kayser	14	Ben Tune
13	Robbie Fleck	13	Daniel Herbert
12	Pieter Muller	12	Tim Horan
11	Pieter Rossouw	11	Joe Roff
10	Jannie de Beer	10	Stephen Larkham
9	Joost vd Westhuizen (c)	9	George Gregan
1	Os du Randt	1	Richard Harry
2	Naka Drotske	2	Michael Foley
3	Cobus Visagie	3	Andrew Blades
4	Krynauw Otto	4	David Giffin
5	Mark Andrews	5	John Eales (c)
6	Rassie Erasmus	6	Matt Cockbain
7	Andre Venter	7	David Wilson
8	Bobby Skinstad	8	Toutai Kefu
16	Stefan Terblanche *	16	Jason Little *
17	Henry Honiball *	17	Nathan Grey *
18	Werner Swanepoel	18	Chris Whitaker
19	Andre Vos *	19	Mark Connors *
20	Albert van den Berg *	20	Owen Finegan *
21	Ollie le Roux *	21	Rod Moore
22	Chris Rossouw	22	Jeremy Paul

Referee: Derek Bevan

Twickenham 31.10.99

New Zealand 31
Tries: Lomu (2), Wilson
Cons: Mehrtens (2)
Pens: Mehrtens (4)

France 43
Tries: Lamaison, Dominici,
Dourthe, Bernat-Salles
Cons: Lamaison (4)
Pens: Lamaison (3)
DG: Lamaison (2)

15	Jeff Wilson	15	Xavier Garbajosa
14	Tana Umaga	14	Philippe Bernat-Salles
13	Christian Cullen	13	Richard Dourthe
12	Alama Ieremia	12	Emile Ntamack
11	Jonah Lomu	11	Christophe Dominici
10	Andrew Mehrtens	10	Christophe Lamaison
9	Byron Kelleher	9	Fabien Galthie
1	Carl Hoeft	1	Cedric Soulette
2	Anton Oliver	2	Raphael Ibanez (c)
3	Craig Dowd	3	Franck Tournaire
4	Norm Maxwell	4	Abdelatif Benazzi
5	Robin Brooke	5	Fabien Pelous
6	Reuben Thorne	6	Marc Lievremont
7	Josh Kronfeld	7	Olivier Magne
8	Taine Randell (c)	8	Christophe Juillet
16	Daryl Gibson *	16	Ugo Mola *
17	Tony Brown	17	Stephane Glas *
18	Justin Marshall *	18	Stephane Castaignede *
19	Andrew Blowers	19	Arnaud Costes *
20	Royce Willis *	20	Olivier Brouzet *
21	Kees Meeuws *	21	Pieter de Villiers *
22	Mark Hammett *	22	Marc Dal Maso

Referee: Jim Fleming

Paris 24.10.99

South Africa 44
Tries: Van der Westhuizen,
Rossouw
Cons: De Beer (2)
Pens: De Beer (5)
DG: De Beer (5)

England 21
Pens: Grayson (6),
Wilkinson

15	Percy Montgomery	15	Matt Perry
14	Deon Kayser	14	Nick Beal
13	Robbie Fleck	13	Will Greenwood
12	Pieter Muller	12	Phil de Glanville
11	Pieter Rossouw	11	Dan Luger
10	Jannie de Beer	10	Paul Grayson
9	Joost vd Westhuizen (c)	9	Matt Dawson
1	Os du Randt	1	Jason Leonard
2	Naka Drotske	2	Phil Greening
3	Cobus Visagie	3	Phil Vickery
4	Krynauw Otto	4	Martin Johnson (c)
5	Mark Andrews	5	Danny Grewcock
6	Rassie Erasmus	6	Richard Hill
7	Andre Venter	7	Neil Back
8	Bobby Skinstad	8	Lawrence Dallaglio
16	Stefan Terblanche *	16	Austin Healey *
17	Henry Honiball	17	Mike Catt *
18	Werner Swanepoel	18	Jonny Wilkinson *
19	Andre Vos *	19	Tim Rodber
20	Albert van den Berg *	20	Martin Corry *
21	Ollie le Roux *	21	Darren Garforth *
22	Chris Rossouw	22	Richard Cockerill *

Referee: Jim Fleming

Murrayfield 24.10.99

New Zealand 30
Tries: Umaga (2), Wilson,
Lomu
Cons: Mehrtens (2)
Pens: Mehrtens (2)

Scotland 18
Tries: Pountney, Murray
Cons: Logan
Pens: Logan
DG: Townsend

15	Jeff Wilson	15	Glenn Metcalfe
14	Tana Umaga	14	Cameron Murray
13	Christian Cullen	13	Alan Tait
12	Alama Ieremia	12	Jamie Mayer
11	Jonah Lomu	11	Kenny Logan
10	Andrew Mehrtens	10	Gregor Townsend
9	Justin Marshall	9	Gary Armstrong (c)
1	Carl Hoeft	1	Tom Smith
2	Anton Oliver	2	Gordon Bulloch
3	Craig Dowd	3	Paul Burnell
4	Norm Maxwell	4	Scott Murray
5	Robin Brooke	5	Doddie Weir
6	Reuben Thorne	6	Martin Leslie
7	Josh Kronfeld	7	Budge Pountney
8	Taine Randell (c)	8	Gordon Simpson
16	Daryl Gibson *	16	James McLaren *
17	Tony Brown *	17	Duncan Hodge
18	Byron Kelleher	18	Bryan Redpath
19	Andrew Blowers	19	Cameron Mather
20	Ian Jones *	20	Stuart Grimes *
21	Kees Meeuws *	21	George Graham *
22	Mark Hammett *	22	Robert Russell *

Referee: Ed Morrison

Cardiff 6.11.99

Australia 35
Tries: Tune, Finegan
Cons: Burke (2)
Pens: Burke (7)

France 12
Pens: Lamaison (4)

15	Matthew Burke	15	Xavier Garbajosa
14	Ben Tune	14	Philippe Bernat-Salles
13	Daniel Herbert	13	Richard Dourthe
12	Tim Horan	12	Emile Ntamack
11	Joe Roff	11	Christophe Dominici
10	Stephen Larkham	10	Christophe Lamaison
9	George Gregan	9	Fabien Galthie
1	Richard Harry	1	Cedric Soulette
2	Michael Foley	2	Raphael Ibanez (c)
3	Andrew Blades	3	Franck Tournaire
4	David Giffin	4	Abdelatif Benazzi
5	John Eales (c)	5	Fabien Pelous
6	Matt Cockbain	6	Marc Lievremont
7	David Wilson	7	Olivier Magne
8	Toutai Kefu	8	Christophe Juillet
16	Jason Little *	16	Ugo Mola *
17	Nathan Grey *	17	Stephane Glas *
18	Chris Whitaker *	18	Stephane Castaignede *
19	Mark Connors *	19	Arnaud Costes *
20	Owen Finegan *	20	Olivier Brouzet *
21	Dan Crowley *	21	Pieter de Villiers *
22	Jeremy Paul *	22	Marc Dal Maso *

Referee: Andre Watson

Cardiff 4.11.99

New Zealand 18
Pens: Mehrtens (6)

South Africa 22
Tries: Paulse
Cons: Honiball
Pens: Honiball (3)
DG: Montgomery (2)

15	Jeff Wilson	15	Percy Montgomery
14	Tana Umaga	14	Breyton Paulse
13	Christian Cullen	13	Robbie Fleck
12	Alama Ieremia	12	Pieter Muller
11	Jonah Lomu	11	Stefan Terblanche
10	Andrew Mehrtens	10	Henry Honiball
9	Justin Marshall	9	Joost vd Westhuizen (c)
1	Craig Dowd	1	Os du Randt
2	Mark Hammett	2	Naka Drotske
3	Kees Meeuws	3	Cobus Visagie
4	Norm Maxwell	4	Krynauw Otto
5	Royce Willis	5	Mark Andrews
6	Reuben Thorne	6	Rassie Erasmus
7	Josh Kronfeld	7	Andre Venter
8	Taine Randell (c)	8	Andre Vos
16	Pita Alatini *	16	Wayne Julies
17	Tony Brown	17	Jannie de Beer
18	Rhys Duggan	18	Werner Swanepoel *
19	Dylan Mika *	19	Ruben Kruger *
20	Ian Jones	20	Albert van den Berg *
21	Carl Hoeft *	21	Ollie le Roux *
22	Anton Oliver *	22	Chris Rossouw *

Referee: Peter Marshall

RUGBY WORLD CUP 1999
FINAL

AUSTRALIA
v FRANCE

Saturday 6th November 1999
Millennium Stadium, Cardiff – Kick-off 3.00pm
Official Souvenir Programme £5.00

AUSTRALIA		FRANCE
2	Try	0
0	Pen Try	0
2 / 2	Conversions	0 / 0
7 / 9	Penalty Goals	4 / 5
0 / 0	Drop Goals	0 / 2
12	First Half	6
23	Second Half	6
0	1st Half ET	0
0	2nd Half ET	0

Minutes in Possession

00:14:12	1st Half	00:07:08
00:12:23	2nd Half	00:09:27
00:00:00	1st Half ET	00:00:00
00:00:00	2nd Half ET	00:00:00

Minutes in Opponent's Half

00:21:24	1st Half	00:21:02
00:17:41	2nd Half	00:27:24
00:00:00	1st Half ET	00:00:00
00:00:00	2nd Half ET	00:00:00

AUSTRALIA		FRANCE
58	Rucks Won	42
6	Mauls Won	5
64	Ball Won in Open Play	47
13	Ball Won in Opp's 22	3
35	Set Piece Ball Won	32
29	Gain Line Crossed	28
29.3%	Gain Line Efficiency	35.4%
7	Handling Errors	13
8	Turn Overs Won	3
0	FreeKicks Awarded	0
13	Ball Passed to Wings	7

		Run	Pass	Kick	Tkle
9	George Gregan	1	62	3	0
9	Fabien Galthie	1	35	1	0
10	Stephen Larkham	2	22	16	0
10	Christophe Lamaison	1	17	11	0
18	Stephane Castaignede	1	9	0	0

AUSTRALIA		FRANCE
14 Scrums awarded		
7	Put In	7
5	Won	7
0	Lost	0
0	Infringements/Incomplete	2
0	Awarded in Opponent's 22	0
27 Lineouts Awarded		
13	Throw In	14
14	Won	13
1	Lost	2
0	Infringements/Incomplete	0
0	Awarded in Opponent's 22	4
28 Penalties Conceded		
12	Conceded	16
9	Conceded in Own Half	9
	06.11.99 17.23.07	

* denotes substitute played

Tackle the issues...

It's not just about the Internet any more. It's about enabling your company to realize the full *potential* of the Internet. It's about managing the *rules* that drive your business. It's about *maximizing* every customer interaction.

Pegasystems' eCRM solutions are rules-driven and Internet architected, enabling clients to compete at Internet speed, achieve a deep level of customer intimacy and perform with *remarkable* efficiency.

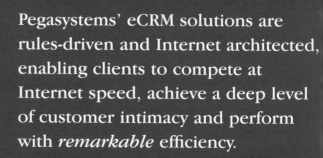

Pegasystems—
Superior Solutions for
Customer Relationship
Management

PEGASYSTEMS

European Head Office
Apex Plaza
Reading, Berkshire RG1 1AX, UK
☎ +44 (0) 118 959 1150
🖷 +44 (0) 118 959 1174

World Wide Web
www.pegasystems.com

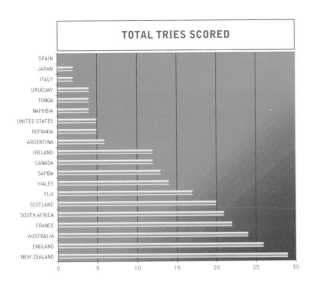

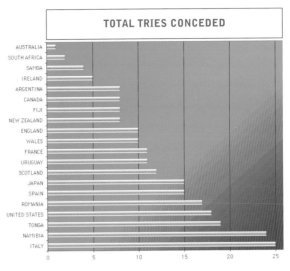

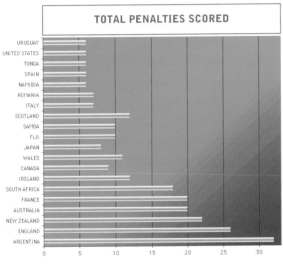

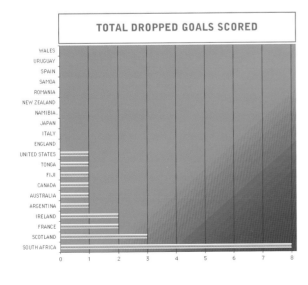

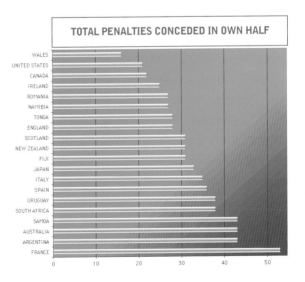

GAINLINE EFFICIENCY - PERCENTAGE CROSSED

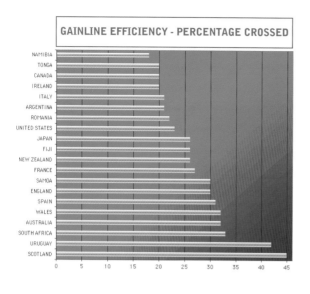

AVERAGE BALL RECYCLED PER MATCH

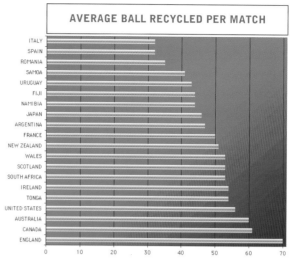

AVERAGE TURNOVERS WON PER MATCH

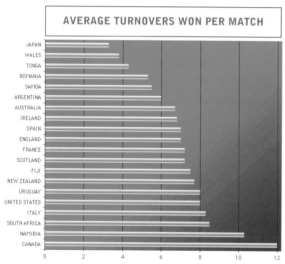

AVERAGE BALL TO WINGS PER MATCH

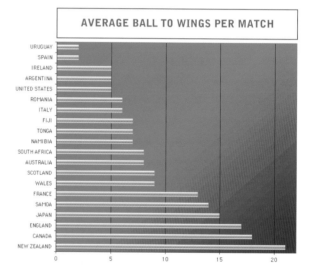

AVERAGE HANDLING ERRORS PER MATCH

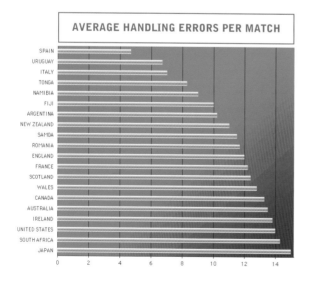

AVERAGE BALL WON IN OPPONENT'S 22

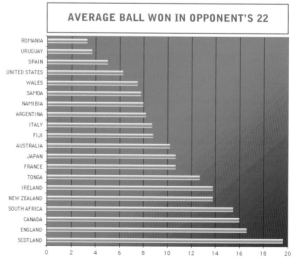